How to Be a Great Student

Kimberly Hatch Harrison

SOCRATICA

The events and conversations in this book have been set down to the best of the author's ability, although some names and details have been changed to protect the privacy of individuals.

First paperback edition April 2021
ISBN (paperback) 9798719535470
ASIN (e-book) B08SKR444S
Published by Socratica
www.socratica.com

For my teachers.

Table of Contents

INTRODUCTION

So. I wasn't always a great student. Don't get me wrong, I went to all the best schools[1], and I got all A's for a long time—like 10 straight years. But it wasn't because I was studious. I was just a really smart kid. That was me getting by on cleverness.

This is the story of how I eventually hit a brick wall and had to learn—fast—how to actually study.

How did I do so well in school? I read obsessively from an early age. I also loved puzzles, and so I always did well on a certain kind of test. My whole life, I was off the charts on all the standards like the Stanford-Binet, the ISEE, the SAT, the GRE. With very little effort, correct answers would flash into my mind. It was easy for me to coast until I found myself, at age 13, at one of the best college prep schools in the country.

For the first time in my life, I was asked to *think* about what I was studying. I should put "studying" in quotes, because up until that time, I really didn't do any proper studying at all. All through grammar school, I sat in class, causing no trouble, trying to avoid getting teased, and then wrote whatever I wanted on tests. Somehow I was always correct.

I showed up at my swanky, elite prep school freshman year and was *immediately* in over my head. I had NO idea how to manage my time,

---

[1] Polytechnic School, Caltech, Princeton

write essays, study for tests—none of it. I was unprepared and ineffective in class, never knowing what was coming next. I'd occasionally copy down what was on the board, but I never reviewed my notes. I would turn in homework completed at the last minute. I crammed for every test.

Don't get me wrong—I wanted to do well, really I did. I'd sit for hours staring at my textbooks, willing the information into my head. Sometimes I'd do well; sometimes I wouldn't. I had no idea how to influence the whole experience. For the first time I realized what it meant to struggle academically.

One of my teachers—God Bless You Eric Stelter—took pity on me. He saw me trying to cram chemical formulas by brute force into my unpracticed brain the day before a test in his class. I had no idea how long it would take me to study for the test, or how to know if I was actually learning the material. I thought it was pure chance how well I would do on his test the next day.

He took my chemistry book from me and flipped to the Practice Test at the end of the chapter (why didn't I know to look there?) and said these magic words:

"Only study what you DON'T know."

Following his instructions, I took the practice test, got a 50%, and only reviewed the questions I missed. I took the test again, and got about 85% correct. I reworked those last tricky questions one more time, and the next day I got a 100% on the real test.

First technique learned: *Only study what you don't know,* by using a practice test. I call it **Smart Test Prep**. I learned the rest of the tips in this book the hard way, by doing absolutely everything wrong. I used the slowest, most painful, most inefficient ways to study, until I figured out much better methods. These saw me through the rest of prep school and college. I have 15 tips to share with you in this book.

If you read one chapter a day, you'll become a Great Student in just a couple weeks.

Eric Stelter is no longer with us. But I'm here to pay it forward. This is what I've learned about how to learn.

Kimberly Hatch Harrison
Los Angeles, California

CHAPTER ONE

How to Prepare Your Study Space

I'm Generation X, a Latchkey Kid raised by Silent Generation parents. My hard-working mum was an immigrant to this country who ran her own small clothing store without any help (not counting me, after school and on the weekends). My father spent his days driving back and forth across Los Angeles as a chauffeur. In other words, my parents were busy doing their own thing. It's not really possible for my parents to have been *less* involved in my studies when I was a kid. It wasn't just my parents who were hands-off, either. Remember, this was pre-Helicopter Parents, pre-Tiger Moms, pre-Soccer Moms. There was a clear divide between the Adult World and the Kid World, and as far as my parents were concerned, school was part of the Kid World. They had no inclination to be in the PTA, or help me study, or give me advice about college[2]. So it seriously BLEW MY MIND when I went over to a friend's house one day and the first room I walked into was... The Study Room.

That's right. This family had turned their entire living room into a dedicated place for their kids to study. Maybe that's normal in certain circles, but I had never *dreamed* of such a thing. I gaped. I really did. I turned around open-mouthed, just like in the movies, taking it all in. There was a big clean table in the middle of the room with a bowl of fresh oranges. There was a computer station. Bookshelves with hardcover reference books. There were maps for studying geography on one wall, and diagrams of how to write Chinese characters on

---

[2] We call ourselves **First Gen**—the first in our family to go to college.

another. It was basically a classroom, right there, taking up a quarter of their house.

I learned something that day that I've never forgotten. It's one thing to *say* education is important to you. But are you living your life that way? If someone walks into your home, or looks at your dorm room, is it clear at first glance that education is a priority for you? Forget for a minute what anyone else thinks about your house—what sort of message are you sending *yourself*?

If you are *really* serious about being a Great Student, you need to create a productive workspace that lets you focus on your studies.

First question: Where? Not everyone has an entire room in a house at their disposal. If space is an issue, don't worry. Your study area doesn't have to be big. It just has to be *dedicated*. Really, all you need is a table and a chair.

But I like to study lounging in bed, you say. *You're wrong,* says I. That's how I used to study, before I went over to Amy Wong's house[3] and my eyes were opened to the error of my ways. Your bed is for SLEEPING. I have insomnia, and I certainly wasn't doing myself any favours by doing homework in bed. Also, just look at yourself, slumped over, sitting on papers. This is bad for your back and bad for your papers.

Pick a quiet space in your room—away from the door and away from the window, if you're on a loud, busy street. The goal is to minimize

---

[3] Not her real name. But close.

distractions. Measure how much space you have, and then find a simple sturdy table and chair that fits the space. Doesn't have to be fancy or even new. Check the local Goodwill and Craigslist. Don't feel like you have to buy something sold specifically as a desk. Any sturdy table will do. When I was in grad school, I bought myself a cheap picnic table. It gave me enough room to spread out all my papers, and even have a place for my whole study group to work together.

Once you have your desk in place, decide what you need to put on it. Your computer or laptop, of course. But what else? Remember, this is a special place *just for studying*, so resist the temptation to start using it for your mail and laundry and dirty dishes and other things you need to put away. The organizational expert Marie Kondo says you need just a few categories of items on your desk: Books, Papers, Miscellaneous Items, and Sentimental Objects.

Books

You should only have the books you need for your current classes on your desk. Everything else should be put away on a bookshelf. If you're not sure whether you'll need a certain book, put it away. If it turns out you have to go get it while studying, leave it at your desk. It's earned a spot there.

Papers

Papers tend to replicate, scatter, and take over every inch of your workspace. To tame your wild papers, take the time to organize them into binders, one per class. Get in the habit of labeling your class notes, your homework, and your tests so it's very clear where each paper should go when you're finished working on it.[4] If you get yourself a set of bookends, you can prop your books and notebooks up vertically, and that will take less space on your desk. It's much easier to pull out what you need that way, too.

Miscellaneous—aka Office Supplies

Office supplies just make me happy, so I indulge myself a little here. The miscellaneous items I need include pens, highlighters, sticky notes, and flash cards. I don't want that all strewn across my work surface, but I do want to keep them at my desk so they're in easy reach. Get a little box for all these doodads, or organize them into a drawer. The point is, you don't want to waste time hunting around to find these essential items when you should be studying. I use all of these specific office supplies when I study, but you might use a different set of tools. Don't clutter up your desk with anything you don't actually use.

Sentimental

Finally, pick *one* sentimental item—a framed photograph, or a soft toy—something that is special to you and, as Marie Kondo says, "sparks joy." A thoughtful friend gave me a beautiful piece of rose quartz, and right now, that's what's taking up a small amount of space on my desk. It makes me happy each time I see it and pick it up. I may swap out my sentimental item next month, but I never have more than one, and that helps make it special. If you have a dozen

---

[4] This can be as simple as writing the name of the class and the date on every paper. It's up to you how to file papers away—for instance, simply keeping them in chronological order, or maybe grouped together by material for each test (UNIT 1, UNIT 2, etc.).

little trinkets on your desk, it's not sentimental anymore, it's just clutter.

THE ESSENTIALS

- Sturdy desk and chair
- Books you are currently using
- A binder for each class
- A box or drawer of office supplies
- A sentimental item to make you smile

BONUS ITEMS TO CONSIDER

- A whiteboard for working out problems or your to-do list
- A planner or calendar
- A potted plant

Note to the reader: the e-book version of "How to Be a Great Student" contains many many live links to recommended resources - books, videos, office supplies, etc. I've created a page for these links on our website, Socratica.com so you won't miss out:
socratica.com/books/great-student
You can follow this QR code to visit the resources page directly:

Have you seen our study tips series on our Socratica YouTube channel? I wrote, filmed, and edited this video series. Don't be alarmed that it isn't me in front of the camera. These videos star my friend and muse Liliana De Castro, who (like me) is a giant fan of reading, studying, and unlocking your brain. She embodies the spirit of Socratica, and celebrates lifelong learning with more concentrated oomph than I could ever muster on camera. Liliana is a big reason this series exists, and I am so thankful we are in the same timeline.

Liliana on set at Socratica Studios

CHAPTER TWO

How to Take Notes

If I had one wish for myself, I'd wish I could start high school over, knowing what I know now.

...Sorry, that's a big fat lie, there's no WAY I would go back to being a teenager. *Rough.* It was rough. But I do think back and shake my head about the years I wasted, struggling in school, when I could have gotten a lot more out of my education with far fewer tears. Had I only known.

I wish I knew, for instance, how to make the most of my time spent in the classroom. Wow, was I completely lost there. Some days I'd be right there with the teacher, following along. Other days, I'd get confused, and by the time I straightened out the problem in my head I had lost several minutes, and had no idea what we were talking about now. Most importantly, I never learned that essential skill: how to distill down lectures into notes, so I'd have something to refer to later. Did everyone flail around as much as I did? Was I out sick the day they taught us how to take notes?

Enter Walter Pauk, professor of education at Cornell who literally wrote the book (*How to Study in College*[5]). Pauk knew that students had a much better chance of retaining information if they not only heard it, but also wrote it down *while thinking about the material*

---

[5] I learned that students use this as a textbook in college courses on "How to Be a College Student." They absolutely did not offer anything like that at my college. Nothing close. Not a whisper. If anything, we were supposed to pretend we knew everything already and were just there for our health.

critically. He invented a system of note-taking that was so successful it came to be known as **Cornell Notes.**

Cornell notes are *not* a word-for-word transcript—they're just the key points, organized, prioritized, and ready for you to study.

This would have solved my biggest problem—I could never write fast enough to take down *everything* my teachers were saying. But no one ever told me I shouldn't! For one class that I took very seriously (AP Biology, my true love), I even used a tape recorder so I wouldn't miss a single word. Susan Grether's lectures were pure gold, full of wit and wisdom. I would painstakingly transcribe the notes, *verbatim*, each night after class. I did very well in that class, but it could have been so much easier and efficient had I known to use Cornell notes.[6]

How do Cornell notes work? It's a 3-stage system of digesting and recording lectures. You divide your paper into three sections: A large column on the right, where you'll take notes in class. A smaller column on the left, where you'll write "cues" to help you navigate through your notes. And finally, a small section at the bottom of the page, where you'll write a brief summary. You can buy pre-ruled paper with these special margins, or you can easily make your own by drawing two lines on each page with a ruler.

---

[6] Full disclosure: my high school best friend Erika Katz (brilliant, underappreciated in her time) tried to tell me I was being crazy. I wish I had listened. You were right, Erika, you were SO right, as you were about so many things.

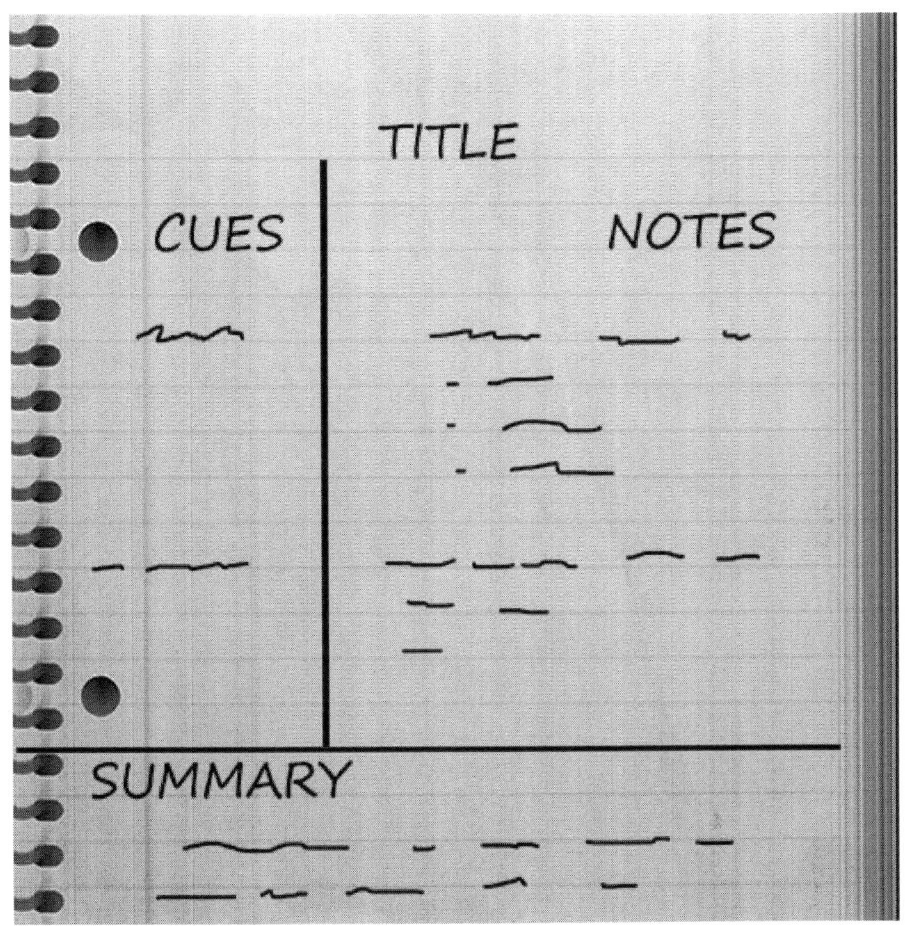

Two lines transform a blank page into Cornell Notes.

What do you write in these three sections?

1) NOTES SECTION

In class, your instructor speaks (for the most part), in complete sentences. That's a good thing. Their sentences are grammatically correct, because they want to be understood. But that's *not* a requirement for your notes. In fact, writing down everything, word-for-word, is almost pointless. It means you haven't done any *thinking* about the material yet—at least, not in any way that you could tell by looking at your notes.

Think *outline*, not transcript.
Your notes in the main section should only capture the key phrases of the lecture.

Abrv!
Use abbreviations wherever you can. For instance, rather than writing the entire sentence: "World War II began in 1939 and ended in 1945," you write "WWII 1939-1945," or even "WWII 39-45." Many words can be left out of each sentence, and you will still understand its meaning.

Bulleted lists are also great.

- Simplify
- Simplify
- Simplify

Leave room.
Skip several lines between sections, in case you need to add details later. In any case, leaving space allows you to quickly read your notes. Now is *not* the time to scrimp on paper.

2) CUES SECTION

After the lecture—and not too long after[7]—review your notes. That's when you start filling in the **Cues** section in the left margin. Use this area to write brief headlines to help yourself navigate your notes. For instance: Causes of WWII. Economic repercussions. Propaganda.

---

[7] I recommend doing this every day when you get home. It's a great way to put the day to bed.

These cues will help you quickly find these sections in your notes when you are working on your homework, or when you need to jump to a particular section to study for your test (remember—STUDY WHAT YOU DON'T KNOW).

3) SUMMARY SECTION

The last part of your Cornell Notes, the **Summary** at the bottom of the page, should be filled in at this point as well. By thinking of how to sum up, in a couple sentences, that whole page of notes, you are doing an impressive amount of learning. You are digesting the material in a way you might not have, were you not asked to summarize the gist of this page.

Bonus: you'll be amazed what a jumpstart reviewing your notes gives you on studying for tests. It's so easy for us to forget what we heard, just a few hours ago, without refreshing our memories. Just wait until you hear about the "Forgetting Curve."

Here's another way Cornell Notes will improve your studying. Remember I told you about my transcripts of AP Biology class? Before I learned the Cornell Notes system, each lecture took up about 20 pages. Years later, I *taught* AP Bio, and made a brief set of notes for myself. Each class period required, on average, 5 pages of Cornell Notes. Think how far ahead of the game you are, if you only have 5 pages of distilled notes to review, instead of a 20-page transcript.

The Cornell Notes method is powerful and efficient. It encourages you to focus on essential details during the lecture, when you take notes in outline form. And since you have to do a quick review to write the cues and summary sections, it has the first round of studying built in.

CHAPTER THREE

How to Read Your Textbook

I spent my entire childhood reading. This was the priceless gift my mum gave to me—she *accidentally* taught me how to read when I was about two or three. She read the *Reader's Digest*[8] to me each night, and pretty soon I was reading along with her. By the time I entered the local Montessori preschool at age three, I surprised everyone by reading on the school schedule that Friday was "Ice Cream Day." What flavour of ice cream, I demanded to know. It was mint chip. I agreed that this was a fine place for me to spend my days.

Once a week, they walked us like little ducks, holding hands two-by-two, to the school library. There, we were each allowed to check out one picture book. This was a pleasant novelty for me—I had never seen so many books in one place. When we returned to class, I quickly finished my book and asked if we were going back the next day. "No, *Wednesday* is Library Day." I informed my sweet golden-haired teacher, Ms. Linda Herring, that I would need to go every day. Lucky for me, Ms. Linda appreciated my spunky self-starter attitude and allowed me to check out FIVE WHOLE BOOKS from then on. I meted out the precious books to myself, one each school day, and by the end of kindergarten I had read the entire school library.

---

[8] I would recommend this publication to anyone studying English. Perfect little nuggets of clear writing.

My parents shared the attitude of so many immigrants—that education was the way to a better life. Alarmed by tales of drugs, gangs, and lazy students, they refused to put me in our local public school. I honestly don't know how they managed to scrape up tuition (they would have sooner DIED before they took charity), but they found a way. I started grammar school at Towne & Country, a private school that offered a safe, if indifferent, education. They did not have a library. My mum, ever my literacy hero, walked me over to the Main Branch of the Pasadena Library and signed me up for a proper library card. The Pasadena Public Library has a giant kids' room and quietly watchful, encouraging librarians. The library became my second home, and still brings me great joy to this day.

It wasn't until I was in the 4th grade that I saw my first real textbook. Up until that point, all of my reading was purely for pleasure. Teachers wrote lessons on the board, they were completed in class, in unison, and when the school day was over, that was it, we were free. At the start of the school year, quirky Mr. Esquivel[9] handed out copies of a glossy book about world cultures, and I flipped through it at random. I came upon a bit about a boy my age in Guyana cooking a pepperpot. *That sounds delicious,* I thought. That's all I remember learning about the subject. I don't think I cracked that textbook for the rest of the year, except when we would occasionally read aloud from it in class. We certainly weren't assigned reading to be completed at home.

---

[9] I honestly can't remember his name. I'm hoping one of my classmates sees this and reminds me. He was a bit nonconformist, with a predilection for starting and abandoning ideas like "let's all fix this rusty bicycle as a class project."

In the 5th grade, Mr. Whitmore (a kindly, proper gentleman who wore his hair in a style from the 1940s and a tie every day) gave me one math textbook and one English book (a reader with about 30 short stories). I took the English book home and read every story that night. Again, that book was only used for reading aloud in the classroom. My math book was purely used for math exercises we worked together as a class. I never took my books home to do "homework." I started to think homework might be a myth made up for television sitcoms. This pattern continued for the rest of my grammar school education.

I was astounded when I entered Pasadena Polytechnic School in 9th grade—by the end of the first day I had at least seven legitimate textbooks. A Math book. *Three* History books. An English book about composition, as well as *Macbeth*, the first of several literary works we would be dissecting that year. A Spanish book. A General Science text. I had reading homework assigned in every class, due the next day.

I took my books home, and diligently read through everything assigned, taking not a single note. I came back to class the next day, and was shocked to find every teacher expected me to be able to discuss what I had read. I could barely *remember* what I had read. I thought I was the best reader in the world. Fact was, I had *zero* textbook reading skills.

I didn't know I was missing basic skills, and so I didn't know how to ask for help. My parents were not plugged in to my experience, and my teachers didn't realize how underwater I was. Gradually, slowly, painfully, I learned how to use these bulky books. I came to understand, with time, that there were predictable, helpful sections in textbooks, including introductions, summaries, and glossaries.

Textbooks are now my friends and loyal companions. Let me explain how to make the most of them.

The most important lesson I learned was that textbooks were not storybooks. With a novel, you crack it open to the first page, read it from left to right, top to bottom, and then turn the page. You continue in this fashion until you reach the end of the book. You never flip back to review what happened earlier. There is no need. A novel carries you safely along, page by page, depositing you at the end with the entire story intact in your mind.

When I read a novel, I enter a kind of dreamy reverie. It's one of the most pleasurable things I do for myself. I can easily read for an hour, feeling mentally refreshed afterwards. Reading a well-written novel is almost as good as taking a vacation. Textbooks, by contrast, expect you to show up ready to work. You must be prepared to do some heavy lifting.

Approach a new textbook like you would a new town. First, you have to find your way around.

The **Table of Contents** is your map. It lists the topics of each chapter, which gives you a simplified, bird's-eye view of everything the book covers. There's a more detailed directory at the end—the **Index**—sort of like an address book that tells you on which pages you'll find very specific subjects. These two tools are often ignored by novice students, but those in the know understand they are meant to be used almost every time you open the book.[10]

It's time to tackle your first reading assignment: a chapter in your new textbook.

1) Find the chapter in the Table of Contents.

First, open the book to the Table of Contents. Read the title of the assigned chapter, and then quickly read the titles of the other chapters. This will help you understand the context of your reading. It's not the entire subject—it's one small section.

2) Feel out the size of the chapter.

Turn to the assigned chapter. I like to count pages, holding up the section I have to read in my hands, just to get a feel for how much work I have in front of me. This way you'll get a sense for how quickly you need to get through the material. If it's only 10 pages, I can read that comfortably in under an hour. If it's 40 pages, I'm going to have to set aside more serious time—and probably not read quite as carefully, if I'm being honest. There are only so many hours in the day.

---

[10] There's a bonus resource at the end of some textbooks: the **Glossary**. Does your textbook have one? A well-written glossary gives you a leg up by supplying you with all the jargon the authors use throughout the text. Often you'll see words in a chapter in boldface. Those are essential terms that you must understand if you hope to do well. Protip: turn the glossary words you don't know into flashcards (see Chapter 8).

3) Preview the Chapter by Reading Section Headings

While reading a novel without spoilers is essential for enjoyment, I'm going to recommend the exact opposite for textbook reading. You want spoilers. You NEED spoilers. Otherwise, every single thing you read will come as a surprise, and on every page you'll be momentarily bogged down by the shock of this brand new information. Here's how you do it: *preview the chapter*. Read all the **section headings** in the chapter, before you read the text. See all those bold headings that start each section of the chapter? Read those before you do anything else.

Don't worry if these section headlines don't make a lot of sense to you. Some textbook writers are better than others at making these headings understandable on their own. You don't need to fully understand what all the headings mean yet. You're just getting these topics in front of your eyeballs, so you'll recognize them when you do your actual reading. Think of them like signposts or milestones. You'll be happy each time you see another one appear, as you work your way through each section of the chapter.

4) Preview the Chapter by reading picture captions, diagrams, and graphs.

There may be pictures or diagrams in your reading assignment. Have a look at these as well. You don't have to dwell on them. Just quickly get an idea of what each picture shows, and read the captions. Again, it's helpful to know what material is coming. You don't have to wonder if there is a useful diagram that ties in with the text—you'll know.

5) Preview the Chapter by reading any summary sections

Anything else before you start reading for real? If you're lucky, there might be a short **Introduction**, and maybe even a **Chapter Summary**. These are EXTREMELY helpful, and I encourage you to read them twice—first before you read the chapter, and again once you have finished. Don't be alarmed if your reading assignment is missing these sections. You'll just have a little extra work summarizing the chapter for yourself.

6) READ and TAKE NOTES.

Finally. It's time to start reading the entire chapter, page by page.

Don't do this empty-handed. Have a pen in your hand.

Notice I said "pen," and not "highlighter?" I do use a highlighter, sparingly, if I come across an important definition or an essential equation I know I have to learn by heart. But that's the exception. **Generally, it's *way* more useful to take notes while reading than to highlight what you've read**. Remember the chapter you just read about Cornell Notes? Time to put that technique to work.

Those section headings are about to come in handy again. They now become your "cues" for each section of notes. I do recommend simplifying these headings as much as possible. For each section, take minimal notes in your own words, using abbreviations and bulleted lists where you can.

When you reach the end of each page of your notes, you'll summarize what you've covered. Continue until you're finished with your assignment, and then re-read the chapter summary. Does it accurately sum up what you just read? Make a note if you think they left out anything really important.

TEXTBOOK READING TECHNIQUE SUMMARY

1) Find chapter context in Table of Contents
2) Count pages to read
3) Preview Section Headings
4) Preview Pictures, Diagrams, and Captions
5) Preview Summaries
6) Read while taking Cornell Notes

This may feel like a lot of extra work, and it is, compared to just reading straight through the text as fast as you can. But **the work you put into note-taking while reading gives you a huge advantage later, when it's time to study for a test.** By taking notes, you are creating a much shorter reference document. You'll be able to leave your textbook behind entirely, relying solely on your few pages of notes.

Doesn't it feel better to know you have just 5 pages of succinct notes to study, rather than 40 pages of textbook to re-read?

CHAPTER FOUR

How to Use a Planner

I started using a planner purely for social engagements. I was in theatre productions in high school, and I needed to know when to show up for rehearsals and performances so I didn't get fired.That meant a special trip to my favourite place in the in the world, Vroman's Bookstore,[11] to pick out something pretty. I preferred the small spiral-bound planners from Sierra Club that showed one week on one side, and a gorgeous nature picture on the other side. They cost TEN WHOLE DOLLARS but I convinced myself my purchase was doing something good for the environment.

I wrote in all of my musical performances, my friends' birthdays, and days off from school in my planner. I left it open on my desk at home so I could glance at it occasionally. There really wasn't much to check, but it made me feel quite grown up.

It wasn't until I turned sixteen, when I was taking all AP classes and had a job in a biology research lab, that I started writing *everything* in my planner. I carried it with me everywhere. Otherwise I was going to *lose my mind.*

---

[11] Southern California's oldest and largest Independent bookstore (founded 1894). This just in—I just learned I can have my book for sale at Vroman's on their Local Authors shelf. Lifelong goal unlocked, dying of happiness.

I mark junior year in high school as the time when I fully grew into a responsible student. I had to, or I would have failed out of my Fancy School.[12] AP Classes meant everything was taught at the college level. I had the standard hours of English, History, and Biology reading to do each night, but I also had nightly Math problem sets, weekly English papers, Spanish translations every other day, Biology lab reports...not to mention the TESTS in every class that I was learning to take seriously. I wrote it all down in my tiny planner in tiny letters, and I began to think that Sierra Club didn't understand just how busy a teenage girl could be.

I was on the right track, documenting due dates. But **I was missing a key idea about my planner: using it to PLAN**. And it was right there in the name, too. Poor little me, so earnest, so clueless.

Nowadays, I use an extra-large Moleskine academic year planner—no pretty pictures, just big sections where I write down due dates, with plenty of extra room for planning. This planner shows me one week on one side, and a large empty space on the other side for to-do lists. This works for me, but you may have different needs. Do you like to see a whole month at once? You might prefer one of those giant desk blotter calendars. Pick a planner that suits your life.

I recommend you use two different colours of ink to write in your planner. I use red for important dates, but you might prefer something friendlier like pink or turquoise. In any case, pick a bright colour of pen that stands out from the regular blue or black that you'll use for everything else.

---

[12] My father's words, as in, "What do they teach you at that Fancy School???"

Start by writing down essential dates (I had that part right). Get out your syllabus for each class, and copy down all the dates of your tests and deadlines for major assignments.

Now here comes the magic part.
Are you ready?

COUNT BACKWARDS from your due date.

That's it, really, that's the big secret of using a planner. By counting backwards, giving yourself enough time to do your work properly, you'll completely eliminate the possibility that you'll leave your work until the last minute. No more cramming for tests. No more pulling all-nighters to write papers.

For instance, you see in your syllabus that you have a test in Chemistry class on Friday that covers the first four chapters of the book. How long will it take you to study for that test? I'd give myself *at least* 4 days, one for each chapter, plus an extra day to review everything all together. So start counting backwards.
Thursday - Final Review
Wednesday - Review Chapter 4
Tuesday - Review Chapter 3
Monday - Review Chapter 2
Sunday - Review Chapter 1

Write down these assignments for yourself in your planner. Otherwise, you'll put it all off until Thursday. *You know it's true.*

This last example was easy—it was already broken into 4 easily manageable chunks for you. What about something less obvious, like writing a paper? If you have a paper due in a week, how do you know how to plan for that?

Again, let's count backwards.
Paper due Friday
Thursday - give yourself an extra day, just in case something goes wrong.
Wednesday - Finish final draft
Tuesday - Get feedback and revise
Monday - Finish rough draft
Sunday - Start rough draft
Saturday - Finish research and outline
Friday - Start research and outline

Again, write all this down in your planner.
If you've never spent a whole week working on an assignment, you'll be amazed how easy and luxurious this feels. No rushing, no worrying. I know there's this romantic notion about staying up all night, waiting for inspiration, but the truth is, your writing will be much better if you give yourself enough time.

PROTIP: Stagger your work.

Use your newfound awareness to spread your work out, especially when it comes to studying for a test or working on a big assignment. You can't let a big project interfere with your other homework and reading assignments. Plan to do a couple Pomodoros for these bigger projects each day—that will help you figure out how far to count back in your planner. What if you have two major assignments due on the same day? Finish one of the projects a day or two early. It's your responsibility to find the time!

I'm going to stop here, because this is the beginner-level intervention for using a planner. If you're a typical high school or college student, this may be all you need.

If, on the other hand, your life is still chaos, spiraling out of control, I suggest you watch our video about Time Management. That video is about using a planner for people who have crazy lives. I hope that's not you, but if it is, we'll do what we can to help.

CHAPTER FIVE

How to Use the Pomodoro Technique

Pomodoro means "tomato" in Italian. I would not have guessed that I would spend so much time in my adult life saying *tomato, tomato, tomato* to everyone. Really, I just won't shut up about it.

It's because **this technique, more than any other study tip, changed my life.**

Not just my life as a student. My life as a human being.

I owe a lot of my success in life to a little tomato-shaped kitchen timer. That's where the Pomodoro Technique gets its name, coined in the 1990s by Francesco Cirillo. Cirillo personally offered consulting and training on how to use this time-management tool. It's a beautifully simple idea.

When I was a sad, overworked high school student, I never knew how long an assignment would take. I would just start it and work straight through. I refused to go to bed until I finished my homework. I could tell I was getting less and less done as the night went on, but I didn't know how to fix it. I used to spend hours, literally HOURS chained to my desk, reading chapters in a History textbook.[13] It's because I'd get distracted, my mind would wander, and I'd have to go back a page or two to actually digest what I was reading. At the end of one of these sessions I'd be completely exhausted, both mentally and physically. I was wrecking my health by not being smart about my studying.

Before learning the Pomodoro Technique, I might tell myself I spent all day Sunday studying for a test, when in fact a good part of that time was spent staring into space or chasing my cat. The truth is, it probably never should have taken more than four hours of concentrated studying for any high school test. I could have given myself most of Sunday off, had I known how to be more efficient with my studying.

I have a pretty good attention span—I can read for what feels like hours. But that's when I'm in the zone, and generally that only happens when I'm reading something I love. What about mundane tasks and dull work, or even worse, the jobs I hate to do? How do I stay focused when I'd rather be doing anything else?

Most of us can stay focused on a task for 20 to 30 minutes, max. After that, our minds begin to wander. It's not a personal failing, it's

[13] History assignments were the worst for me—I could *not* remember anything I was reading. The one exception was my History of Science and Technology class taught by Dr. Nate Feldmeth. Everything in that class came alive for me, and I learned the importance of *context* and *themes* for reading history. My History Hero. Years later he officiated our wedding ceremony.

just a normal part of being human. The Pomodoro Technique works from this assumption that your brain NEEDS a break after about 20 minutes. So you *plan your work with these breaks built in.*

POMODORO TECHNIQUE: Work, break. Work, break.

1) Pick a task you need to do. Set a timer for 20 minutes. Now: go. Do this task for 20 minutes, and don't let ANYTHING interrupt you.
2) At the end of the 20 minutes, take a break! You've earned it. Take a real break, now. Get up from your desk, walk around, drink some water, maybe get some fresh air.
3) After a short break of about 10 minutes or so (you'll get a feel for how long you need), set your timer again. Do another 20 minutes of CONCENTRATED effort.
4) Take another break. Repeat these cycles until you finish your task.
5) If it's a really big job, give yourself a longer break after 4 Pomodoros. Go for a walk, or have some lunch. Then continue with your task, again, in 20-minute chunks

One surprising thing you'll find about the Pomodoro technique: you'll be so much more efficient! You'll get more work done in less time. What's more, you won't feel nearly as tired afterwards, because you respected your need for mental and physical breaks.

Here's how to make this technique into a studying superpower: Keep track of how many Pomodoros it takes you to do each task. You have a reading assignment? Make a checkmark in your planner each time you do a Pomodoro, until you finish. Now you know it takes you about three Pomodoros to read a chapter in your Biology book. You have a math problem set? Two Pomodoros. Now you know how much time you're going to need for the *next* assignment. No more guessing. After I learned the Pomodoro Technique, I suddenly had a tool to monitor the time I was *really* working.

How long should your Pomodoro sessions be? Personally, I like 25 minutes on, 5 minutes off. But you do you. Play around and figure this out for yourself. **It's better to go shorter rather than longer. You want to feel like you could keep working when your timer goes off.**

Now I use the Pomodoro technique for *everything.* I use it when I'm writing. I use it when I'm editing videos. I use it when I do my laundry. It's especially good for all the things I hate to do and used to put off—I'll say to myself I'll do one Pomodoro, and then I'll stop. Most of the time I finish that thing I was dreading.

Shout-out to my Pomodoro writing buddy, fellow teacher, and soul-sister Charity Hume who generously offered her insights and advice as I wrote this book. Charity and I write together almost every day. We set a timer for 25 minutes, and WRITE. We take a little break, talk about how it went, and then do it again. We both wrote books during the 2020 PandemicTime, almost completely during our Pomodoro sessions.[14] This technique really, *really* works.

---

[14] Charity's PandemicTime book was *The Naked College Essay*, which demystifies the college application essay. I can also enthusiastically recommend her book of writing exercises: *The Path to Creativity - Creative Writing Exercises to Awaken the Artist Within*. Visit charityhume.com.

CHAPTER SIX

How to Study for a Test (aka Smart Test Prep)[15]

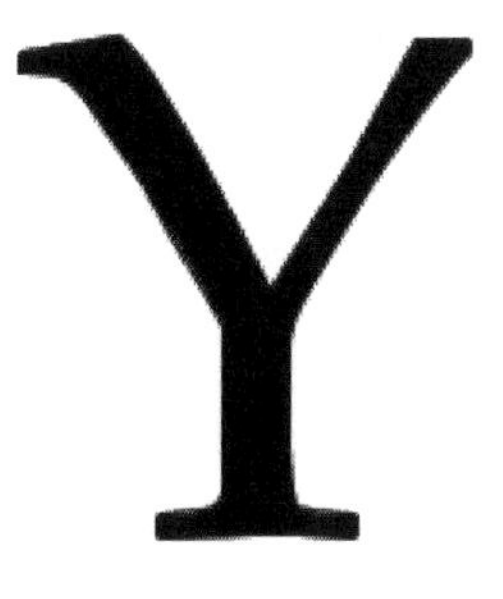

ou have a test coming up, and you're panicking.
You *don't know* how to prepare.
You *don't know* what will be on the test.
You *don't know* what will happen when you fail.
You *don't know* how you'll ever get over this.
Student life is torture!

ENOUGH.

I can't believe how mythologized tests are. Everyone builds them up to be this terrible, scary thing. I'm convinced it's because of the uncertainty. *You don't know what you don't know.*

The solution: self-testing.

If you're actually studying properly, you should be self-testing all the time.

I mean ALL THE TIME. So much so, that any given test shouldn't faze you in the slightest. Well, okay, tests that your instructor gives in class are going to be higher-stakes than your self-tests. But if you do enough self-testing, you won't get anxious about the real tests anymore. *I promise.*

---

[15] This is by far the best chapter in this whole book, btw—I'm telling you right now.

Before I learned this **Smart Test Prep** method (as described in the Introduction), I wasted endless hours studying, with mixed results. Whereas after incorporating this technique, I would typically only spend about four hours studying per test, which meant my other work didn't suffer. What's even better, I always knew just about how well I would do on the test. **Smart Test Prep** really, *really* works.

And here it is, my foolproof, highly efficient method:

SMART TEST PREP

Step 1: Narrow down what you have to study by taking a pre-test.

Yes, before you start any kind of formal review or studying. That's why we call it a PRE-test. I know this sounds strange. Maybe you've never done it this way before. Please give it a chance.

If your instructor hasn't given you a practice test, and there aren't any sample questions in your textbook, you can look online for a test about the subject. Another option is for you and your classmates to get together and make one on your own. Do a survey of all the major topics, picking questions from your homework and ideas that came up in class. Don't get caught up in the weeds, asking "gotcha" trivia questions. Stick to the big ideas.

Now. Set a timer for an hour, and take the pre-test. Don't agonize over any of the questions. You're doing this to quickly figure out what you *don't* know. As soon as you finish the test, grade it.

Are you worried about how poorly you did? That's not the point, at all. Maybe you missed 50% of the questions on the pre-test. That's okay. It means there's 50% of the material that you *don't* have to study. That's better than okay—that's great! You've already cut your studying time in half.

Next, focus on improving. **Your score will only go up if you devote time to the material you don't know.** You know what won't help your score? If you keep studying the material you already know.

Step 2: Make a list of topics to study, based on the questions you missed.

You will only study the topics you got wrong on the pre-test. I know this will feel weird to the uninitiated. We love getting questions right—it gives us a little pleasurable dopamine hit. You have to wean yourself off of that nice feeling you're accustomed to, and adjust to the unpleasant reality. This is the whole point of pre-testing: it lets you narrow down what you have to study. And that feels great, once you get used to it.

Step 3: Gather all your study material together.

You'll need:

- your class notes
- your assignments
- your reading notes[16]

[16] If you've taken good reading notes, you won't need your textbook—except if it has a practice test.

Step 4: Only study what you don't know.

Give yourself a day where you re-read your class notes—that is, the parts that are about the topics you missed. Look for those topics in your reading notes and homework assignments, too. Do you understand what you got wrong on those questions now? If not, ask a friend to help you out here. Make sure to help them in return.

Step 5: Retake those missed questions.

Did you get them all right? Are there any you still just don't get? If you've reviewed, asked friends, and are still puzzled, now's the time to bring in the big guns. Ask for some assistance from your TA, your tutor, or your instructor. Don't show up empty-handed—there's a proper way to ask for help. Read Chapter 10, on How to Use Office Hours, and prepare before you go.

If there's enough time, repeat this process. Take another practice test, review what you got wrong, and then re-take those questions. You should see an improvement on each practice test, and you'll do even better on the actual test.

SMART TEST PREP SUMMARY

1) Pre-test

2) Review the questions you missed

3) Re-test on the missed questions

4) Repeat as needed

I have a *lot* more to say about studying for tests—this is just an overview. In future chapters, we'll talk about specific techniques in detail: Flashcards, Mnemonic Devices, Feynman Technique, etc. For now, repeat this mantra:

ONLY STUDY WHAT YOU DON'T KNOW.

CHAPTER SEVEN

How to Improve Your Memory

I remember the *dumbest* things.

I remember the cast from every play I ever did. Oh, yeah, that's *really* going to come in handy, in case I have to round everyone up for one more performance, 30 years later.

I remember the theme songs from every 1980s TV show. When will *that* ever help me in life?!

I remember my mum's business phone from when I was in kindergarten, and we all had to memorize our contact info in case we got lost. Don't believe me? 213-681-1841. That number hasn't been in service since my mum retired in 1998, but it's still in my head, just in case.

There are also many sad and scary things I remember. For instance, I saw *way* too many horror movies when I was a little kid in the 70s.[17] The visuals haunt me! I wish I could remove those images from my mind.

Remembering a lot of useless junk is one thing—I'm mildly annoyed that there's a lot of clutter taking up space in my head. But then there's the opposite, extremely frustrating experience: when you KNOW that you know something, and you just can't pull it out from the depths of your mind. One time I looked right at a girl I had known for a whole year and could not think of her name. Thanks a LOT,

---

[17] It was impossible to escape—It was the Golden Era of horror films in the movie theatres and "Elvira, Mistress of the Dark" on TV. I spent a lot of time peeking from behind the sofa.

brain. How many miles in a kilometer? GAH. C'mon, brain! I need that one!

If only we could *control* what we remembered.
I don't have a magic pill to make you forget bad things. But I do have some good techniques for the things you *want* to remember. Or in the case of school, the things you HAVE to remember.

If you're feeling skeptical or, worse, feeling down on yourself that you can't remember everything,
STOP RIGHT THERE.
Let me set you straight.
Your brain forgets almost everything ON PURPOSE.
Really.[18]
Your eyes and ears (all your senses) are taking in SO much information, constantly, that one of the chief jobs your brain has is to throw out almost all of that information and distill what's left down to a manageable load. Some of that will be saved in our short-term memory, and even less will make its way into our long-term memory. This is perfectly natural, and while we don't fully understand it yet, researchers are starting to pin down the mechanisms of memory. Some memory loss is undoubtedly inescapable—it's just biology.

Where does this leave us, as students? Do we have *any* say in the process? How can we tell our brains not to throw something away, but to keep it because it's really important?

The first technique to improve your memory is exactly that.

---

[18] Trust me. I'm a scientist.

TELL your brain that you want to remember something.

I know, it might feel silly, but making the effort to deliberately start a memory is surprisingly effective. When you study, take a moment and tell yourself, "I will remember these 10 pages." Or simply: "Remember this."
Say it with confidence. You're in charge.

Now, I'm not going to pretend like that one technique will take care of everything. We're going to layer on multiple techniques. The more ways you exert yourself to remember something, the less likely it will fall through the cracks.

The second technique to improve your recall is to create **mnemonic devices.** Mnemonics (from the Greek word for "memory" or "remembrance") are tools that help us remember. You take the thing you want to remember, and make an acronym out of its first letters, or make a sentence out of the words. There's usually a pattern or theme that's easier to remember than the original thing you're trying to keep in your head. This technique is especially useful if you're trying to remember a list in a specific order. It's hard to define mnemonics in one sentence, because they come in various forms. Let me share a few examples:

My very educated mother just served us nine pumpkins.
This is a funny sentence I learned from my kindergarten teacher, Ms. Linda Herring, that helped me remember the order of the planets in our Solar System:[19]

---

[19] Back when Pluto was still a planet.

Mercury
Venus
Earth
Mars
Jupiter
Saturn
Uranus
Neptune
Pluto

Note that the sentence makes sense grammatically, and it's funny. Both of these things make it easier to remember than the original list. If instead I tried to use "Mumble Vacuum Electricity Marbles Jump Salmon Up Nowhere Parthenon" it wouldn't be very much help as a mnemonic device—there's no reason for those words to be in any particular order since it's not a real sentence, and doesn't make any sense.

Roy G. Biv

This is another mnemonic I learned from Ms. Linda. It sounds like a man's name, but really it's an abbreviation of all the colours of the rainbow, in correct order:

Red, **O**range, **Y**ellow, **G**reen, **B**lue, **I**ndigo, **V**iolet

Apparently, I learned a LOT of useful info in kindergarten. Also, this might help convince you that mnemonics really do help information stick in your head, sometimes for the rest of your life.

That's not to say mnemonics are just for kids. It's a challenge for commuters in Los Angeles to remember the order of the streets running downtown. From East to West they are: Los Angeles, Main, Spring, Broadway, Hill, Olive, Grand, Hope, Flower, Figueroa.[20] A classic mnemonic used by native Angelenos is "In Los Angeles, there's a Main Spring on Broadway. Walk up the Hill to pick an Olive. Isn't it Grand to Hope to find a Flower on Figueroa?" I like this one more: "Los Angeles is where my dreams will come true. The Main thing, I say with a Spring in my voice, is I'm gonna star on Broadway before I'm over the Hill. I was born to play Olive Oyl. I'll be Grand, at least I Hope. For my stage debut, bring Flowers but please, no chocolates—I've gotta watch my skinny Figueroa." Remember, *humor helps.*

This little tour across downtown L.A. reminds me[21] of the next kind of memory aid: "**Mind Palace,**" or **"Method of Loci."** This technique dates back to the scholars of ancient Greece, so you know it's stood the test of time. You tell yourself a story[22] about walking around a very familiar place—for instance, heading down your hometown's Main Street, where you know every shop in order. At each location, you mentally place something you want to remember. Again, this is especially useful if order matters.

Here's a challenge that's perfect for the mind palace technique. Memorize the 12 British Monarchs in order: Queen Anne, George I, George II, George III, George IV, William IV, Victoria, Edward VII, George V, Edward VIII, George VI, Elizabeth II.

---

[20] What about Alameda, you say? No need to include it. No one could ever forget Alameda. It's where they keep the nuclear wessels.

[21] hehehe

[22] Our brains *love* stories.

I'll start you off. We're going to be traveling through Disneyland (or you can pick some other place you're really familiar with, like your house). You walk through the front gates of Disneyland, and stop at the giant Mickey Mouse flower planting. Standing there is Queen Anne, angrily digging up the planter, hunting for a Queen Ant. She's shouting "I'm the only Queen Anne around here!"

Next you start down Main Street, and you stop in the Magic Shop. There's a magical mirror there that you look into and see four copies of yourself. A fancy fellow named George is looking in the mirror, and he sees George I, George II, George III, and George IV. He likes what he sees. "I see FOUR GORGEOUS GEORGES!" he says.

Now *you* think of something for William IV. Choose something funny and weird, because that makes it more memorable. It helps to include a lot of silly details for each step. Also, any time you can make something rhyme, or use alliteration (repeating the same first sound, like "the wind is waving the weeping willows"), that makes it easier to remember.

Another trick is that our brain enjoys it when we sing it a little song.[23] Any time you can make a memory singsong or even slightly musical, you have a better chance of remembering it.

Don't expect your memory to be perfect. Write things down.

[23] There's a good reason for kids to sing the *Alphabet Song, Conjunction Junction*, etc.

The very act of writing things down will help you remember. And then if you happen to forget? That's okay. Because you wrote it down! I had one professor who would say to me, in an irritated tone, "Don't write all that down!" He expected me to be able to listen to him for *hours* with perfect recall, I guess. I ignored him and wrote what I needed. Don't feel bad about using the tools you need.

PRACTICE.

We're starting to learn from memory research that every time you "remember," you're actually re-writing that memory, completing the circuit between relevant neurons. The more times you recall a fact, the more sturdy and reliable the wiring of that brain circuit, and the more durable the memory will be. You'll learn a *very* useful technique for practicing your memories in the next chapter about flashcards.

CHAPTER EIGHT

How to Use Flashcards

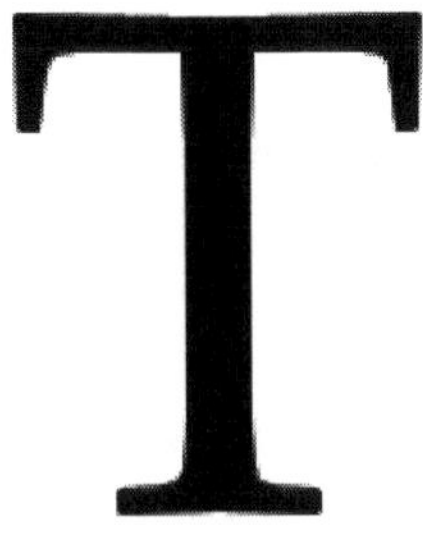

his chapter is about memorizing things fast and efficiently. It's Old School and Low Tech. And it involves one of my very favourite things: buying office supplies! We're talking flashcards, and it's an easy way to turn studying into a game. *You like games, don't you?* Yes, you do. Even if you don't think you do, your brain *LOVES* it when you "gamify" learning.

For this technique, you'll need to buy yourself some index cards. As a penny-pinching kid, I would always buy the simple white 3x5 cards (those were the cheapest) and cut them in half. Twice the bang for your buck! Nowadays, you can affordably buy a variety of different kinds of index cards, some of them precut to small sizes. They even come in different colours.[24] *FANCY!*

Analog or Digital?

Now I realize, some of you are going to want to hear about digital flashcards. I know they're out there. I've used the app that rhymes with donkey[25], and it's just fine, especially for memorizing things with audio files. This is a good option if you're learning another language and you want to practice your pronunciation or test your recognition

---

[24] I'll list some flashy flashcard options in the resources section. But simple gets the job done, too.

[25] ANKI. It's not a secret or anything. I'm just making a joke.

of spoken phrases. But I'm not really interested in endorsing one particular digital platform, especially since apps come and go.

I always come back to analog. Paper and pen. You can use old school flashcards even when you don't have phone service or your battery is dead. One of these two things (if not both) is almost always true for me, so I'm going to talk about good-old-fashioned paper flashcards—the kind you make yourself.

You heard that correctly. You're going to make these **by hand**, not buy them pre-made from some company. The biggest benefit to making your own flashcards using pen and paper is that when you actually write out what you want to remember, you're doing something that digital or pre-made flashcards *can't* do for you. You're creating a **muscle memory** of writing out that information. *You're connecting the thought to something physical in your body.*

You **SEE** the information, while at the same time, you **FEEL** the information, as you are writing it. That's a lot of bonus brain connections you're getting for free. Want to be an overachiever here? **SAY** the information out loud while you're writing. Now you're also using your brain to **SPEAK** and **HEAR**. More brain connections!!

What are Flashcards good for?

I realize that I started hyping up this chapter about flashcards so much that you might start to think this is the One True Study Tip you need to succeed. It is definitely one of the very best study methods, but it's not the right tool for *everything*. For instance, this is not the best way to study if you're solving problems or reasoning things out, like for math class. To be a Great Student, you'll use flashcards in concert with the other techniques in this book. You'll see.

Flashcards are best for when you need to know a set of facts cold—zero mistakes, zero hesitation.

So you'll use them for vocabulary terms, specific numerical values that never change, indisputable historical dates, things like that. It's also great for visual information you need to be able to recognize at a glance: any kind of sign or symbol,[26] chemical structures you need to name, or if you have to memorize the names of paintings for an art history class.

I started using flashcards as a freshman in high school studying Spanish. They *saved my life.*

In Southern California, most kids take Spanish as a second language, and by the time they graduate they can't string five words together. I swear we learned the same simple lessons like "my pencil is yellow"[27] every year for eight years, all through lower school and middle school. My chief memory of the first eight years of Spanish class was this game we played called *Loteria.* It's kind of a Spanish language version of bingo, with drawings to illustrate important words in Spanish like "la sirena" (a mermaid) and "el catrin" (a fancy man). I was pretty scared of the "el borracho" square and would try to cover the drunken man's face with my pinto bean marker.

As I've mentioned before, I moved on to an *intense* prep school for high school. And I started 9th grade taking Spanish II, because,

---

[26] Great for learning Chinese Hanzi or Japanese kanji vocabulary.

[27] See, that's only four words.

obviously, those eight years of Spanish class had to count for something, right? NO. GOD. NO. I could not say *anything*, other than "Mi lápiz es amarillo," or sometimes "Tengo miedo del borracho," when I thought about *Loteria.* Meanwhile, I've got my friend Gail Fernandez in my class who had been speaking Spanish since she was in the womb. I was so screwed. I suddenly had dozens of vocabulary terms to learn every week. I was learning all kinds of "conjugations"—I had never even *heard* that word before. My previous method of studying Spanish (doing nothing and just showing up for class) wasn't going to cut it anymore.

My sweet, encouraging instructor, Laura Pendorf, taught me an essential study technique without naming it. She suggested studying with flashcards, and to just do a little every day. Put the cards into two piles: what I got right, and what I got wrong. On the next day, study them again. A few days later, study again. "You can't learn it all in one day," she told me. She also told me some excellent stories about making silly mistakes when she first started speaking Spanish on a trip to Mexico, including announcing she was "embarazada" (which means pregnant and not embarrassed). I loved her so much!

Years later, I learned the technical name for this flashcard technique: **Spaced Repetition**.

Spaced repetition is a term that came out of memory research (actually, research about forgetting). German psychologist Hermann Ebbinghaus pioneered this research back in the late 19th century. He documented how fast someone forgot a list of made-up words they had memorized. The results were pretty upsetting to anyone who is trying to learn something. Ebbinghaus plotted the results in what is now called "**The Forgetting Curve":**

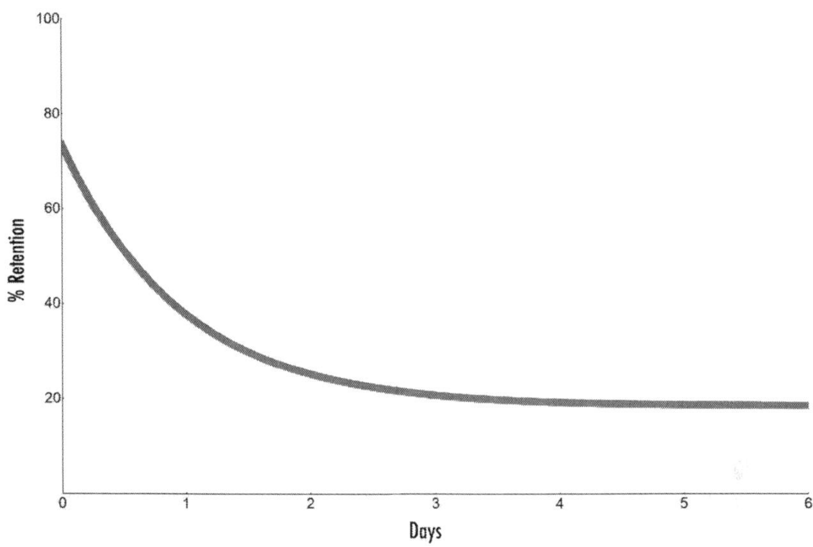

As you see, **we begin forgetting something almost immediately**, even though we *thought* we had safely tucked it away in our memory banks. Those people who think they're going to remember a lecture days or weeks later are *seriously* fooling themselves.

But don't despair! Ebbinghaus didn't just have bad news to report. Importantly, he found that the slope of the forgetting curve could be changed. How? By injecting more exposures to the material. In other words, *studying*.

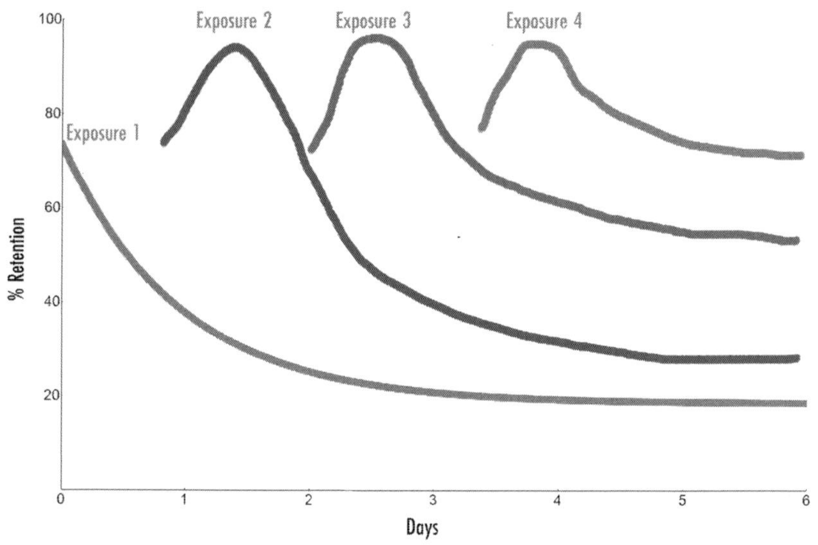

What these results show is that **if you take the time to do some review the next day, you will remember a much greater percent than if you just had one exposure to the material.** Review again the next day, and you'll remember even more. This is "spaced repetition" in a nutshell—don't try to do all your studying in one go. Ms. Pendorf was right! Study one day, let some time pass, study some more, let some time pass, and study again. Three exposures (study sessions) are WAY better than just one. Spaced repetition "lifts up" the forgetting curve so you retain much more of the material.

The "forgetting curve" really *fired up* psychology research for a number of years. So many research papers came out about this idea that I'm kind of shocked that spaced repetition isn't that widely known or discussed amongst the people who really need this information—teachers and students.

So what do the years of research tell us? It turns out, we know pretty much that spaced repetition is the way to go, but we don't know for sure what's the *best* spacing or what's the *best* number of repetitions. There's too much variability to make up one hard and fast rule. For instance, it depends on the kind of material you're learning, and what kind of testing you'll experience. Are you preparing for a short test in one week? In that case, you should probably study on Day 1, Day 2, and Day 6. Are you hoping to remember everything for your end-of-year exam? In that case, it doesn't make sense to do so much studying all in one week, but space it out more over the course of months, like Day 1, Day 2, Day 30, Day 60, Day 120, Day 240.

How long can the spaces be before you forget too much and it's just like starting over? You'll have to figure that out for yourself. But the general principle holds: don't put your notes away and then try to cram all your studying right before the test. Instead, use spaced repetition and break up your studying into three or more chunks. Repeated exposures to the material will really help it persist in your memory.

The Fabulous Flashcard Game

We're going to take the power of Spaced Repetition (that I learned from my Spanish instructor, Ms. Pendorf) and the power of Study What You Don't Know (aka Smart Test Prep that I learned from my chemistry instructor, Mr. Stelter) and put them together to form the **Fabulous Flashcard Game.** It's actually pretty fun, because you're competing against yourself—the worthiest of opponents.

EXPOSURE 1: The first time you read or hear the term. Maybe you're in class, maybe you're reading your textbook. Okay, you've put the info into your brain once, but now we know (because of the forgetting curve) that it's a *race against time* to make sure you don't forget it.

EXPOSURE 2: Make your flashcards. When should you do this? *You saw that forgetting curve.* It's exponential, with an extremely steep drop-off. That means you're forgetting super-fast in the first few hours after you learned something. So do this step *as soon as you can* after you first learned something. If you saw it in class during the day, make your flashcards in the afternoon or evening.

You'll write one term per card, with a term on one side and the definition on the other. As much as possible, these should be in your own words. So don't just copy a long definition straight out of the textbook. Simplify—but don't simplify so much that you lose meaning. Just be succinct. Ideally, say the term and the definition out loud as you write the card. Remember, you're using as many of your senses as you can. The more parts of your brain you enlist, the better.

EXPOSURE 3: Test yourself. When? Let's say the next day. Pick a side. I usually start with the definition, and try to guess the term, because that's usually a simpler thing to remember. Read the definition, and before you turn the card over, try to say the term.

Now be VERY honest with yourself. Did you know the term, without hesitation? If so, put it in the "YES" pile. If you were even a little bit wrong, put it in the "NO" pile.

If you can, do this out loud, but if you have to be quiet, don't use that as an excuse not to practice. Remember, you're interrupting the forgetting process, so you need to get this exposure in and boost that forgetting curve back up.

Count how many cards are in the "NO" pile. You're going to beat that next time!

EXPOSURE 4: Re-test in the other direction. Shuffle all the cards, and this time, look at the term and supply the definition. Remember, be *completely* honest about whether you really know each card. Did you ever hear that phrase "You're only cheating yourself?" It's perfect for this situation. It can help to study flashcards with a friend—pick someone who won't let you get away with anything. How many cards are in your "NO" pile? Did you beat your score from last time?

Now here's where you're going to inject some *Smart Test Prep* excellence to turbo-boost your *Spaced Repetition*. Remember the power of only studying what you DON'T know. You don't want to keep studying that whole stack of flashcards over and over. I know it feels great to get the right answer, but the truth is, it's a waste of your time to keep studying those easy cards. That won't boost your test score. From here on out, you need to focus on what you DON'T know. So you're only going to continue studying with the "NO" pile.

Take those "NO" cards, and slowly read the term and the definition out loud. Say it in a singsong voice. Write a sentence using the term. If it's *still* not in your head, take the time to go back to your class notes or your textbook and re-read that section.

EXPOSURE 5: Last chance before the test. Let's save this for the day before the test. Shuffle the cards and go through them again, looking at the definition and saying the term. Any cards in the "NO" pile? Review those topics, then re-test yourself one last time, just on those few "NO" cards, in the opposite direction (look at the term and supply the definition).

I love the feeling of seeing that pile of "NO" cards get smaller and smaller. The nice part about competing against yourself is that *you always win.* Be sure to give yourself a reward. Nothing big. Maybe just a little hug. Endorphins are nice.

CHAPTER NINE

How to Use the Feynman Technique

"The first principle is that you must not fool yourself—and you are the easiest person to fool."

Richard Feynman

I went to Caltech. This is a strange college in Pasadena, CA—maybe the strangest college in the whole world. In fact, they don't call it a college or university, it's an ***institute.*** The California Institute of Technology is affiliated with almost a hundred Nobel Laureates, and is considered one of the most elite places to do scientific research. It is also home to a very small group of undergraduates—around 200 per class, and that number drops precipitously as the weeks go on in the school year, and students "flame out" from the insane amount of work.

"Techers" are crazy overachievers studying mainly science and engineering. Most Caltech undergrads were the smartest kid in their high school—maybe even in their whole town. You can imagine the psychological impact it has on an 18-year-old kid who based their whole identity on being a STEM genius. They show up at Caltech and they're thrown in amongst a couple hundred people just like them, and they find out they're not the smartest person in the room anymore. On top of that, the coursework is so rigorous that it's not unusual for these genius students to just flat-out *fail*. I was in classes where the average test scores were in the 30s. What does this do to the students? It's generally a disaster. Many of these young brainiacs fall apart under the strain, and if they're lucky, they gradually inch their way back to being okay enough to graduate. About a quarter of my class never recovered. I made it, but I have scars.

I went to college to study biology, but every (and I mean EVERY) student at Caltech took a "core curriculum" of math, chemistry, and physics for the first two years (I just added biology on top, like the idiot overachiever that I am). Essentially, this means that every Caltech student has half of a degree in these subjects. While you are completing your core curriculum requirements, you decide what you want to specialize in, and continue with more advanced courses in that subject.

I'm not going to pull any punches here. My professors at Caltech were NOT good teachers.[28] Most of them felt (or at least acted) like teaching was a giant imposition on their time. They wanted to be back in their labs, working on their cutting-edge research, rather than wasting their time with egomaniacal freshmen. I mean, can you blame them? But they didn't have to be so *nasty* about it. I'll never forget one physics professor GOING OFF on a student who raised his hand to ask a question. He was confused about the derivation of a formula, because he was getting something different than what the professor had

---

[28] I have to include a giant disclaimer here: my Humanities professors were actually quite committed to good teaching. Peter Fay taught me the History of India and the careful interpretation of historical fiction. Louis Breger taught me Psychology and how it informed works of literature. Sigrid Washburn taught me German Language and German Literature and never once teased me about my Austrian accent. John Sutherland taught me to delight in the insoluble mysteries of Literature like "*Who betrayed Elizabeth Bennet*?" Kevin Gilmartin taught me Romantic Era Literature and graciously mentored me through an independent study of William Blake (deeply weird, deeply inspiring). Ritsuko Hirai Toner taught me a year's worth of Japanese in 10 weeks. *Domo arigato gozaimashita!*

written on the board. I had the same issue on my paper, and I had *almost* raised my hand to ask the same question.

"DO YOU THINK YOU'RE CLEVER? DO YOU FEEL GOOD ABOUT YOURSELF MAKING ME LOOK STUPID? OH YOU'RE SOOO SMART!" The weird little man went on like this for several minutes, shouting and turning purple, all the way up to his balding head. All of us shrank back in our chairs. It wasn't until hours after class that I started to get angry. *How were we supposed to learn anything if we were afraid to ask questions?* I forced myself to continue attending lectures, because I was terrified of failing, but I never, *ever* asked a question in that class again.

That professor won a Nobel Prize in Physics a few years later. Figures.

Listen. If your instructors wave off your questions, or make you feel bad for not knowing everything before you've even taken their class, that's them being a BAD teacher. Good teachers encourage the spirit of exploration and curiosity. If they're shutting down your inquisitive mind, you've got to fall back on your own ingenuity. The Feynman Technique is all about making sure you are really learning, even in the absence of a good teacher.

"The Great Explainer"

It's a real sadness in my life that I narrowly missed getting to learn physics from Richard Feynman. Feynman is revered at Caltech, not just as a Nobel Prize winner, but also for dedicating his adult life to teaching physics. He literally wrote the book (actually, a 3-volume set of books) on the subject. Feynman died in 1988, two years before I arrived at Caltech. He was stolen from the world by cancer (as was my beloved mum). Cancer can GET BENT.

Feynman was a real character. He wasn't the product of an upper-crust family or exclusive prep school. He attended a public high school in Queens, but was brilliant enough to go to MIT and then Princeton. These places didn't change him. He never lost his rough New York accent. He avoided jargon, even when teaching the most advanced subjects. Joyous in the classroom, he'd wave his hands like an orchestra conductor. He led an informal meeting once a week where Caltech undergrads could show up and discuss any physics questions they found interesting, like "what colour is a shadow?" Professor Feynman played bongos, and took part in student theatre productions. He studied art—studied anything that he found interesting, which seems to be a little of everything. He wasn't like most Caltech professors who spent every hour in their labs, focused on their own narrow specialty. He was insatiably curious, and found a way to connect with the world.

The Feynman Technique wasn't invented by Richard Feynman, but it *is* named in his honour. His nickname was "The Great Explainer," and this is the heart of the Feynman Technique: **can you channel the great Feynman, and explain something the way he could?**

THE FEYNMAN TECHNIQUE SUMMARY

1) **First, pick your subject.** From your class notes or textbook, pick one small section. You're not going to ramble on about all of biochemistry—you're just going to explain one thing, like photosynthesis.

2) **Next, write a simple explanation of the concept.** SIMPLE being the key here. Imagine you are explaining this subject to a very bright, inquisitive child.
3) **Is there any part that you're struggling to explain? Using lots of jargon? That, right there, is where you need to focus your study.** Because when you really, REALLY understand something, you'll be able to explain it in simple language, even to a complete novice.
4) **Take that hard part (you probably didn't even realize it was giving you difficulty before this exercise), and re-read just that section of your notes and textbook.** See if you can find another explanation somewhere, from a video on YouTube or talking to your TA or instructor. Sometimes you'll hear a slightly different way of putting something, or learn about it in a slightly different context, and that will make it click. Now you'll be able to explain it simply, like Feynman.

When should you use the Feynman Technique? I recommend you use it early and often.

When you are studying a new subject, there is an initial phase where you simply take it all in. Listen carefully in lecture, taking notes. Read the entire chapter in your textbook and don't skip a single figure. But then, you need to turn around and make the subject *yours*. Put it in your own words.

The Feynman Technique is perfect for this second phase of learning. It's a great way to force yourself to be honest about whether you are just parroting back what you were told, or have you graduated to where you *really* understand it.

The Feynman Technique is a kind of self-diagnostic for whether your knowledge is mature and fully integrated.

Practice with your friends, especially if they're not taking this class. They'll be able to tell you whether you're really being clear about the subject. Don't let them be polite and just pretend to understand. *This is for the game.*

CHAPTER TEN

How to Use Office Hours

The first time I went to Office Hours, I was a freshman at Caltech.

It was time for our first test in Physics 1. I had a pretty strong background from my high school AP Physics class. I got an A, and scored a 5 on the official AP test. I wasn't planning on majoring in Physics, but I was determined to do well in this most fundamental of subjects. To understand Biology, you must understand Chemistry. And to understand Chemistry, you must understand Physics. My future as a scientist depended on it.

I worked all hours of the night for a straight week, trying to understand my lectures and homework, trying, trying, trying. As soon as I opened the test, I knew I was in trouble. Unlike my high school physics exams, the problems on this test didn't resemble what we had been doing in class all week. Clearly they expected me to be able to apply what I had learned to brand-new situations. I think I was able to solve two or three of the problems completely. For the others, I wrote down which equations I thought *might* be relevant, tried a few more things, and eventually reached the end of my ingenuity.

When we got back our tests,there was a lot of bragging and joshing amongst the other students. Me, I sank in my seat, devastated.
I had just FAILED my first college physics test.
35%.

How could I have failed?
What was happening??!!
What was I going to do if I failed out of college? What would my parents say? Would I have to go to work in my mum's little shop for the rest of my life?

We didn't go over the test in class. Instead, the professor dived right in with brand-new lecture material. I realized I was *really* screwed if I never got an explanation for the questions I missed (most of them). I summoned my courage and took my paper to my professor's office after class. "I was wondering if we could talk about where I went wrong on the test?"

He was in a great mood, and he took my paper with a smile. "Well, you don't have to worry about your grade, do you," he said, picking up a red pen.
OH *SHEEEEEET.*
I really wanted to say, yes, clearly, I'm failing, I need help, but wordlessly I shook my head.
He started marking a few more areas. "Here, you can assume this mass is a single point. Here, you dropped a negative sign." He took off two more points and handed my paper back. I backed away and disappeared. So much for getting help.

It wasn't until later that the truth came out.
The average for the class was a 32%.
I was fine.
But also, I wasn't. I wasn't making full use of what my school had to offer. I was so terrified of failing, that I was afraid to ask for help even though I really, really needed it. I never went to office hours unless it was an emergency.

As the first person in my family to go to college,[29] I only *vaguely* understood the job of a professor. I just thought of them as someone to be feared and admired. Now I know: aside from writing and delivering lectures, creating meaningful homework assignments, giving constructive feedback on papers, drafting tests, and *endless* grading, instructors also usually offer regular office hours. It's included in the tuition. It's your right as a student to use them! But what are office hours for? They're not for last-ditch prayers for deliverance, as I thought all through my undergrad years. Office hours are there for your instructor to help you when you get stuck. They've been exactly where you are now, and they know how to get you *un*-stuck.

Students and Teachers are Partners in Learning

It wasn't until I started teaching classes as a grad student at Princeton[30] that my eyes were opened to how all this was supposed to

---

[29] Thankfully, many colleges have started offering specialized orientation programs for First Gen students. There's a whole unwritten curriculum that constantly trips up the students who didn't grow up with college grad parents, and they have no one they can ask for help. When college is new to you, you don't even know what you don't know.

[30] Here's something you may not realize about most colleges. Even at elite universities, a lot of the teaching is done by untrained graduate students. We didn't have the slightest idea how to teach! We were just thrown into the deep end with a free copy of the textbook (*yay!*) and an incredible amount of responsibility—and we just had to *deal*. As a true type-A personality, I learned all of my students' names the first day. I was determined to figure out how to help them all to pass. It was grueling work, with a never-ending avalanche of papers to grade. And yet, I caught the teaching bug and went on to teach for a total of twelve years. But that's a story for another book.

work. I learned that (good) instructors actually *wanted* their students to succeed, and were willing to help if you would just ask them.

That's not to say you should show up without doing any work and expect your instructor to perform a miracle. Remember, as the student, you have your role to play. **You have a lot of work to do before you should show up at Office Hours.** Otherwise, it's a waste of your time and your instructor's time.

The most important lesson I learned in my first foray into teaching was that the students and instructors are partners. Successful education only happens if both the teacher and the student are willing to do their part. I had little patience for the students who would show up to my Office Hours and expect me to re-teach my lectures and do their homework assignments for them. But the students who came prepared, showed me what they had tried, and worked with me to succeed? There wasn't anything I wouldn't do for them.

Now that I've seen it from both sides, as both a teacher and a student, this makes perfect sense to me. But I wish someone had spelled it out to me back when I was a struggling student. I didn't know it was okay to ask for help, and I didn't know the best way to ask for help so it would actually be useful, and not a bandaid on a fatal wound.

Dale Corson was a physics professor at Cornell University who knew what Office Hours were really for, and he *did* spell it out to his students. He described this method so well, it is now named after him. This technique was initially intended for his physics students, but it can be applied to any complex subject. Ready? Here it is:

THE CORSON TECHNIQUE SUMMARY

1) You're stuck. That's okay.
2) Stop and do a little self-diagnosis. Is there a keyword you don't know that you can look up in the glossary?
3) You're still stuck. That's okay.
4) Is there a similar problem you worked in class? Re-read it, slowly and carefully.
5) You're still stuck. That's okay.
6) SLOWLY re-read the sentences in your textbook leading up to where you got stuck.
7) SLOWLY re-read your class notes about this subject.
8) SLOWLY re-work similar problems.
9) Take a break to clear your head.
10) Look at the problem again with fresh eyes. Still stuck? That's okay.
11) Ask your study group.
12) Still stuck? That's okay. NOW it's time to go to your TA or professor for help.
13) **MOST IMPORTANT STEP: Document everything you tried, and exactly where you got stuck.**
14) Go to Office Hours and show them your notes. Now they have something to work with.

It's that *documentation* that will win over even the crustiest of instructors. It shows them that you care, that you are invested in your learning, and that you are a willing and able partner in your own education.

Learn from my mistakes, and learn from Dale Corson. Go to Office Hours. Make us proud.

CHAPTER ELEVEN

How to Take a Test

Confession: *I think tests are exciting.*

I've always tested well (except for a few sad days in college), and I think this attitude has a lot to do with it. I've never been afraid to take a test, because it has always felt like the natural culmination of my work as a student. I'm all for learning for learning's sake, but to study and study and study and never take a test feels a little like cooking a five-course meal and never getting a taste, and then going away hungry. Don't you *want* to know how you're doing?

There's a lot of angst and mythology about tests. The phrase "high-stakes testing" brings on much hand-wringing amongst parents and educators alike. Have you bought into the hysteria? Being afraid of being tested is not doing you any favours. People complain that there's too much testing nowadays, and that *may* be true (relative to how much time is spent on instruction), but bellyaching about it isn't going to make you into a Great Student. Making tests into some kind of educational bogeyman is helping no one. Yes, tests require work, and yes, tests often determine your final grade. What's more, it's not possible for a test to completely document everything that you have learned. But that doesn't make them *evil*. When done right, tests are an important part of the learning process.[31]

---

[31] To understand more about the idea that testing can be part of the learning process, read up on "formative assessment."

How can you cultivate a healthy sense of respect for tests, and not freak out about them?

If you've been studying like a Great Student all along—taking good notes in class, keeping up with the reading assignments, taking reading notes, doing your homework, getting help during office hours, taking pretests, studying what you don't know—by the time your test arrives, you'll be ready.

This long list of things you should be doing before the test makes it clear: **Cramming has no place in your life.** If you take the advice in this book seriously, you'll never cram again. Not only will you be too busy to cram, you'll find it's completely unnecessary. If you've been in the habit of studying only the night before tests, it's no wonder you've been stressed about how well you might or might not do. There's just too much work to do before a test, and if you leave it all till the last minute, you're setting yourself up for failure. Make yourself a promise that you won't put yourself in that position ever again.

We've already talked about the Great Student way to *study* for a test, aka **Smart Test Prep** (Chapter 6). I'm assuming you did your due diligence, and you found out the format of the test (how long it is, what subjects are covered, types of questions, etc.). You broke your studying into small Pomodoro sessions. You've taken practice tests, and you have a good feel for how prepared you are. So now, let's talk about how to do your best when it comes time to actually *take* the test.

Set Yourself Up For Success

You don't have to worry about staying up all night cramming—that would backfire anyway, by making you more anxious—so instead, you're going to get a good night's sleep. Before you go to bed, pack up your bookbag with everything you need so you're not rushing in the morning. You should already know what's allowed in the classroom on the day of the test (pencil/pen/calculator/water bottle). Is it an open-notes test? In that case, don't forget your notes!

In the morning, eat a hearty breakfast. Don't choose sugary kiddie cereal that will get you hyper and then let you crash 30 minutes later. Eat some protein and complex carbohydrates for sustained energy, like eggs and whole wheat toast. Fuel up for the battle ahead. It's a good idea to slip a protein bar in your bag, too, just in case your blood sugar drops right before the test.

Give yourself plenty of time to get to your classroom. You don't want to be rushing in at the last minute so you're flustered right before the test starts, or even worse, losing some of your precious test-taking time. Plan to get to the classroom at least a few minutes early, so you can calmly take your seat.

Your Name Comes First

When the test starts, and they hand out the papers, put your FULL name on the top as soon as you get it. I can't tell you how often I had to chase around students after a test, trying to figure out which "Albert" went with which test. Even worse, sometimes a test had NO name. If your instructor can't figure it out, you're going to get a big fat zero. Don't make your instructors work harder than they already do. Every test, every time—FULL NAME.

Read the Instructions

You've taken a practice test or two already, but don't make any assumptions about this test. Read the instructions carefully. You probably have to answer every question, but every now and then you'll come across a test where you can choose which questions to answer. Make *sure* you know the rules of this test. Also, check how long the test is. *Don't skip the last page!* This is another sad test story that happened too often with one or two of my students every year.

Take a look at the clock. Do you have an hour? Should be plenty of time.

You're going to take the test *twice.*

That's right. You're going to make *two* passes through the test, so plan your time accordingly. Generally I like to spend about 15 minutes on my first pass, and then 45 minutes on my second pass. But use your best judgment—not every test is the same.

First pass

Just like how you learned to pre-read your textbook, you're going to pre-read your test on the first pass. **Only answer the questions that are immediately obvious, where you definitely know the right answer.** Circle the questions you're not completely sure about (you'll come back to them on the second pass). By doing this quick first pass, you'll see the scope of the whole test. You'll get a feel for how long you can spend on each question this way—if there are 30 problems, you'll know you can't spend 10 minutes on any one of them. You'll know which are the hard parts of the test, and you won't waste your time on the easier parts.

Pause, Regroup, and Refocus

Take a deep breath, and rest your eyes for just a moment. Take a drink of water. Check the time, just so you are aware how much time is left. *Refocus.*[32]

Second Pass

Now flip your paper back to the start and make your second pass through the test. This time, slow down, and **be very methodical** with the questions that you skipped. Don't reread the questions you answered the first time. *Stay focused.*

STRATEGIES FOR ANSWERING TOUGH QUESTIONS

1) **For multiple choice questions, don't overthink it. After you've eliminated the answers that are clearly wrong, pick the *most obvious* correct answer from what's left**. Don't second guess yourself, and don't get into an argument with yourself about what is the very best answer. Multiple choice questions stress people out so much, I've written a whole chapter about them, so stay tuned for the next chapter if this is a real problem for you.

---

[32] If you find yourself struggling with focus, you may find it helpful to practice meditation. I don't mean *during* the test. Meditation is a daily practice. Think of it as exercise for your brain. Give it a shot.

2) **For math and science problems, SHOW YOUR WORK for partial credit. Most important step: start with the general equation.** For example, write down the general form of the quadratic equation first before you start substituting in values. Don't just write some numbers down—what if they're the wrong numbers? You won't get any credit for that. You need to show that you understand the general principles, and which equations would be useful in this type of problem. The specific numbers are really an afterthought.
3) **For essay questions, make sure you answer the question that is actually being asked**. So many times when grading a test, I'd read a beautifully written answer that I had to give zero points to—because it was answering a completely different question. I know, it's tempting to want to show everything you know. This is not the time or the place, because you'll only get points for what is actually being asked.
4) **If you really are stumped on a problem, don't leave it completely blank**. Write SOMETHING. Jot down any notes that you can think about the subject. Often, just by writing what you do know, you'll jostle something loose in your memory and the relevant information will come pouring out.

Don't leave the test room early.

If you've finished your test and there are still a few minutes left, use that time to check your work. Reread all the questions slowly. You might catch a mistake! Use every minute you have to eke out all the points you deserve. Having said that, however, resist the temptation to change any answers just because you're having second thoughts. *Only change an answer if you've found a real mistake in your work.*

Now go home and *rest.* You worked hard, you did good work. You deserve a break. Take a couple hours off to do something purely fun, and rest your weary mind.

After the Test

Pretty soon, you'll get your corrected test back. Now be honest—what do you usually do with that test, once you've seen the grade? Have you been in the habit of stashing it away and never looking at it again?

Here's one way that Great Students distinguish themselves from the rest of the pack. You're going to use that corrected test to understand yourself, and get even stronger.

But the test is over! you protest.
This test is over, yes, but those problems you missed haven't magically disappeared. **You are still responsible for knowing that material.** It's going to show up again, possibly even immediately in the next unit (lots of subjects build upon what came earlier). At the very least, it's going to show up again on the midterm or final. So you still have a job to do. Remember this from **Smart Test Prep**: STUDY WHAT YOU DON'T KNOW.

If there are any problems you missed, figure out why you missed them now.

Was it just a silly mistake, like misreading the problem? Don't beat yourself up about it, that happens to the best of us. Just take it as a sign that you'll need to slow down and read the questions more carefully on the next test.

Is there something you *really* don't understand on the test? This is the perfect time to go to Office Hours (Chapter 10) and ask your instructor about where you went wrong. Honestly, as an instructor I was so impressed with my students who put in that little bit of extra effort. It made it clear to me that they really cared about learning, and I remembered that when it came time to write letters of recommendation.

Keep this in mind—no test is life or death. It's just one test. There's always another one coming, so get ready.

CHAPTER TWELVE

How to Answer Multiple Choice Questions

"Do you have your Number Two pencil?"
{Wilhelm Scream}

The Multiple Choice Test is something you might be afraid of, but you must face this fear. You *have* to figure out how to do well on this kind of test. There's no getting around it.

You may feel like multiple choice tests with those bubble forms are impersonal. Most big schools rely heavily on those automated scantrons, because there's simply no way to grade all those tests by hand for all the thousands of students that are enrolled. And why would you, honestly—what a waste of a teacher's valuable time. There's nothing *personal* about correcting a test question marked A,B,C,D, or E. That doesn't mean picking the right answer isn't a true measure of your personal understanding. Your progress as a student can, indeed, be captured in a snapshot by a multiple choice test.

Multiple choice tests have gotten a bad rap, and that's probably because it's not the right kind of test for *all* occasions. There are some situations where an essay question makes more sense, like if you're being asked to make a logical argument about something. In a science class, completing a lab exercise might be a better expression of your understanding of *some* topics. But for many (maybe even most) situations, the multiple choice test is the perfect way to isolate what you do and don't know, and where your understanding breaks down.

Multiple choice tests are often the best tool for deciding whether you can make fine logical distinctions between closely related ideas. If you don't want to believe that, if you're inclined to argue—I want you to stop and take a good, long look in the mirror. Have you been fooling yourself about how much you know, and how well you know it? *Do you object to multiple choice tests because you're just not very good at them?*

One reason why people hate multiple choice tests so much is that they expose your weaknesses. They can find all your soft tender mushy parts and rip them wide open for anyone to see. You might be embarrassed. That's okay. It can be very uncomfortable to face up to your deficiencies. But you MUST root out all the weak spots if you really, truly want to be a Great Student.

I was lucky. I saw, early on, how powerful multiple choice tests were as a way to find out for myself what I understood, and where I needed more work.[33] Doing multiple choice practice tests is the heart of what I came to call **Smart Test Prep**. And it was through that self-testing that I got to be really good at taking multiple choice tests.

I think it all comes down to practice. The more multiple choice tests you do, especially in the comfort of your own home with the pressure off, the better you'll feel about taking them as real tests that count for your grade. They'll lose their novelty, and become just another tool at your disposal.

---

[33] Read the heartwarming account of my academic awakening in the Introduction to this book.

The Power of Self-Testing

This is where we'll start. **The first thing you must do to get better at multiple choice tests is to take them, often, and in a low-stakes setting.** That means incorporating them into your normal study routine. Are there practice multiple choice questions in your textbook? If not, I suggest you go looking for some. You can ask your instructor if they have any practice tests (this might be a long shot, but worth a try). You can also look online, although it's hard to find something that perfectly aligns with what you are studying in your specific class. If you do find a practice test online, use your best judgment about which questions are actually relevant for your studies.

Write Your Own Test

If you find yourself without any practice multiple choice questions, you'll just have to make them up yourself. Team up with some of your classmates, and create a practice test together. You may actually find it challenging to come up with good questions—they can't be too easy, or it won't be a good test of whether or not you learned the material. "Gotcha" questions are also not helpful. Believe it or not, good teachers don't want to trick their students. Put them to the test, yes, but not cheat them out of the grade they deserve.

It wasn't until I was teaching at Princeton, and had to come up with my own multiple choice questions, that I saw there is something of an art to it. By writing your own questions, you'll become hyper-aware of things like the special vocabulary used, like *always* or *never*. You'll also learn that it's a dead-giveaway when several answers are saying essentially the same thing. They can't all be right, unless the answer is indeed (E), all of the above.

Now that you have your practice test, it's time to...PRACTICE. Treat this test just like you would a real test, except I don't recommend taking it under strict time constraints. You don't want to be stressed while taking this practice test. Use the "two-pass" system we discussed in the previous chapter. Go through the test quickly on the first pass, answering only the most obvious questions that you definitely know the answers to. Circle the questions you're not sure about. Take a brief break, rest your eyes, then start your second, slower, more methodical pass through the test, going back to the questions you skipped the first time.

Grade your practice test. *Don't feel bad if you missed half the questions.* 50% is actually the number I was rooting for when I used this technique. All I really hoped for was that I retained about half of the material *before* I started studying in earnest. Remember, this **Smart Test Prep** way of studying is the best way of narrowing down what you actually have to study. The trick is to only study what you DON'T know.

I'm now going to share the most common problems and issues I saw my students have when they took multiple choice tests. Any of these sound familiar?

COMMON PROBLEM 1: READING COMPREHENSION

Carefully examine the questions you missed. Was it because you read the question too quickly? Here's something that happened all the time when I was teaching: a student would raise their hand during a test, saying they were confused by a question. I would never give them the answer. Instead, I would just read the question outloud to my student, and they'd say "Ohhhhhh!" Half of the challenge is slowing down, reading for comprehension, and thinking about what the question is actually asking.

COMMON PROBLEM 2: THE PROCESS OF ELIMINATION

Here's another issue I often saw my students have: they'd narrow down the possible answers (good) but then they'd argue with themselves about the remaining answers (bad). If you find yourself hedging and fudging about one of the answers, saying, "but, sometimes, maybe, in just the right conditions, this *could* be right, if you look at it in a certain way"—that's not what a correct answer feels like. When considering the possible answers on a multiple choice test, you should be looking for the answer that is pretty much always correct.

COMMON PROBLEM 3: RELUCTANCE ABOUT GUESSING

On your practice multiple choice test, if you come across a question where you can't eliminate a single answer choice, that's a strong signal that you have to study that material before your real test. That's great! But what if that happens to you during the real test? You're going to have to GUESS. *That feels so strange.* But that's exactly what you should do, unless there's a "guessing penalty."

I had some students who simply *refused* to guess, even though that meant they now had zero chance of getting the question right. Why the reluctance? I suspect it's because they were overcome with scruples and didn't want to get credit for something they didn't really know. However, there's a chance your subconscious mind *does* know the right answer. By guessing, you're giving your subconscious the chance to help you out.

Any tricks about guessing? There's some folk wisdom out there, like (E) is the most commonly used correct answer choice. *Maybe*? Personally, when writing multiple choice tests, I found I had to work hard to not automatically write the correct answer first, followed by a bunch of increasingly ridiculous wrong answers.

Other common ways to guess include looking for those special qualifying words, like *all, always, none,* and *never.* It's often easier to write that answer, and so as an insider, I'm telling you that could tip the chances towards that being the right answer. You'll get a feel for this by writing your own practice multiple choice questions.[34]

I hope at the very least you can achieve some peace and equanimity about taking multiple choice tests. It's no use being in denial about the importance of these tests—they're going to be with you for your entire academic career—not to mention their vital significance in the form of standardized tests like the SAT, ACT, AP, GRE, MCAT, LSAT....Doing well on those multiple choice tests can make a huge

---

[34] I just realized, at the end of this chapter, that most of my advice about multiple choice tests comes from my experience as a teacher, rather than as a student. I learned how to do very well on multiple choice questions while I was a student, but I don't think I could have articulated how I did it. Aside from simply being exposed to hundreds of practice questions, I think it was the experience of writing my own multiple choice questions that really, finally, fully demystified the multiple choice test for me. This is another great reason why you should start writing your own practice multiple choice questions.

difference in your career options going forward. My wish for you is that you don't let them stand in your way. And if you take what I have written to heart, you'll find that multiple choice tests will actually help you achieve Great Student status.

CHAPTER THIRTEEN

How to Improve Your Writing

When I turned 12, my mum bought me a typewriter. I'm talking a good-old-fashioned manual Smith Corona that had a satisfying *DING* at the end of every line, a *brrrrtszzzz* carriage return, keys that jammed, and everything. If I close my eyes, I can still smell the ink from the black and red ribbon. This is how deeply *Gen X* I am—in my grammar school, starting in the 4th grade, they put us in typing class Mondays and Wednesdays, and computer class Tuesdays and Thursdays. Here we stand, with one foot in the past and one foot in the future.

I'm actually truly grateful that I learned how to "touch type" (our classroom typewriters had no letters on the keys, so we had to memorize the layout of the keyboard). It's a skill I still use every day. Our delightful elderly typing instructor, Walter Neff,[35] made up his own humorous practice sentences our class would type in unison. One was, "No, Mason, we will not be typing with our noses."[36] Humor can go a long way towards keeping schoolkids happy—look how I still remember that one joke. How *starved* we all were for the slightest bit of humanity from our teachers.

---

[35] Probably a relative of the famous architect Wallace Neff. This was Pasadena, after all.

[36] Mason McClure was one of my classmates. We all thought this was hysterically funny. Lesson learned: whenever possible, include the names of your students in your handouts.

I set my beloved typewriter up on a rickety card table that swayed every time I pulled the carriage return, and felt very grown up and important. I used that typewriter to write demand letters (more like very polite request letters) to my mum's customers who were behind on their bill. I used it to write all of my papers in high school. I used it to fill out college applications, and a few years later, I used it for the very last time to fill out grad school applications. It sits on a shelf in my closet now.

Why don't I get rid of that old dinosaur?
I owe that typewriter a lot. It taught me how to write!

Technology has come a long way since I was 12. I've survived about ten versions of Microsoft Word, and now I write using Google Docs. My words are immortalized somewhere in The Cloud, and I can play with every sentence, every word, endlessly, without wasting a bit of paper or having to replace a typewriter ribbon. There's no risk of losing your work anymore—"versioning" means that earlier drafts are kept safe for you, whether they're worth anything or not.

Photographers who learned to shoot on film cameras established good habits of framing and composition, because they didn't want to waste a shot. Film was expensive, and it was too much work to develop shoddy pictures. I'm glad I learned to write on an old-fashioned typewriter. It taught me the importance of thinking ahead and planning my writing, so I didn't have to retype everything because I had second thoughts.

Back in the day, if you made a mistake while typing, you had two choices: either 1) use white out correction fluid, wait a minute for it to dry, type over it, and hope that was the only mistake, or 2) start all over with a fresh piece of paper. Option 2 was the way to go, obviously, if your correction was anything more serious than a wrong letter or two. If you wanted to rearrange paragraphs, that *definitely* meant typing the whole thing over again from scratch. Before word processors, some people went to extreme lengths to avoid retyping, including pulling out a pair of scissors and some tape to put their thoughts into better order.

The best way to avoid retyping a page, of course, was to *plan out* what you wanted to write.

I learned the art of which sentence goes where from my high school English teacher, Bill Pickering.[37] He was the first person to carefully read my writing, rip it into its component parts, and show me how to put the pieces back together into a stronger, fiercer Frankenstein's Monster that lived and breathed and conquered.

Before I studied with Pickering,[38] all the instruction I had ever received about writing was really just about *grammar*. Personally, I love rules of usage—when to use a comma or a dash. How to properly use apostrophes. When to use "which" or "that." Those are all great, fun puzzles.[39] But it's not really advice about *writing per se*, as when we say, "she's such a good *writer*." Although good grammar

---

[37] I took a lot of English classes, but Bill Pickering is the only one I remember actually *teaching* me. Because of him, I am a serious reader and a serious writer. I am forever in his debt—a happy place to be.

[38] The mark of a Great Teacher: you think about them by their last name. Feynman. Pickering.

[39] If you'd like to learn more about English Grammar, we made a whole playlist of topics people commonly struggle with.

is essential for good writing, no one is thinking about how Jane Austen really knew her way around a semicolon.

To put it into math language, good grammar is *"necessary but not sufficient."* If your essay is riddled with grammar mistakes, it makes it hard to focus on your good ideas. But perfect grammar on its own doesn't make for a well-written paper. After you master grammar, you need to learn how to best express your ideas. But before I started high school, I had absolutely zero instruction on the principles of composition.

For instance, it was a brand-new idea to me that you should think ahead of time about how to start an essay. After that first brilliant opening sentence, what comes next so you don't lose your audience? What should you save for last? Examining how to present my thoughts before I started a writing assignment didn't just save me from tiresome retyping. Take a little care in this direction, and suddenly your writing is persuasive and compelling.

I'm talking about the idea of **rhetoric**, of course—it's not some secret knowledge. These rules of composition have been handed down from ancient times. Whole books have been written on the subject, and if you want to be any kind of writer of distinction, you'll want to steep yourself in these concepts. See the resources listed at the end of this book and on socratica.com for some recommended reading.

For our purposes, to whip your writing into shape in short order, I'm going to give you the cheat codes for improving your compositions. You don't have to be an extraordinary writer to pull this off. You just have to be careful and deliberate. Ready?

1) Pre-writing and Brainstorming

First, get your raw ideas out on a piece of paper. You're not worried about writing beautifully *yet*. That's why this pre-writing stage is often called "brainstorming"—it's a messy process. Actually, I want to pull back from that idea a bit. "Brainstorming" has a weird, loosey-goosey, *woo-woo* aura around it. Most people treat it like you are tapping into some precious mental treasure trove, and you have to be very careful not to scare any of the genius ideas away. According to common wisdom, you're not supposed to use *any* judgment and you write down anything and everything you think of on the page.

I REJECT THE COMMON WISDOM!

Time is short, my friends. If you start with a big platter of random kitchen scraps, how're you going to make a cake? You want, at least, to be selecting eggs, flour, butter, and sugar before you start cooking. Common sense, right? I'm all for turning off that part of your brain that constantly tells you your writing is lousy.[40] But there's no reason to turn off your brain *completely*. When you pre-write, you want to wind up with something you can actually use.

To that end, I suggest that you **title your brainstorming page.** If you're writing an essay about how the internet has affected our attention span, write that at the top of your page. This is a message to **stay focused on this one topic.** Everything you write on your brainstorming page must pertain to the question at hand.
It might look something like this:

---

[40] See our video about Impostor Syndrome

<u>THE INTERNET HAS AFFECTED OUR ATTENTION SPAN</u>

Distracted all the time   short attention span   can't read a whole book   can't watch a whole movie   don't remember what you just read   need to look at your phone all the time   using a phone in the movie theatre   using a phone while you watch TV   Older generations still read books   Did this start with the internet or is something else happening   ADHD diagnoses up   Did "factoids" in newspapers pre-date the internet?   Average length of magazine articles getting shorter   Look things up with Google rather than remember them   We have to use GPS or we get lost because we can't remember directions   No one remembers phone numbers   How much of this is smart phone vs internet   Can our brains recover?

2) Find brainstormed clusters to pick your main points

Hopefully, the ideas on your brainstorm page will naturally cluster into a few sub-topics. *Distracted, short attention span, lowered reading comprehension, poor memory.* It looks like you're going to be arguing that the internet has not done us many favours. Good. Now you can sum all that up in a thesis statement: "Exposure to the Internet has made our attention spans shrink." This will be the heart of the first paragraph of your essay. If there are a handful of minor points on your brainstorming page that don't quite fit, leave them out. The more unified and coherent your points are, the harder it will be to find fault with your paper.

3) Each brainstorm cluster gets its own paragraph

This is where your brainstormed clusters will do a lot of the composition work for you. Each paragraph usually starts with its own topic sentence, so sum up the gist of each idea cluster to form this sentence. Then the sentences that follow explain what you mean in more detail. In the body of each paragraph, you can include examples, give evidence in the form of data, or a quote from an expert. Most importantly: **stay on topic.** If you find yourself starting a new idea, that's when you start a new paragraph.

4) Sentences should proceed logically.

After every sentence you write, think about what information should naturally come next. If you're explaining to someone how to make a traditional pound cake, you would write something like this:

STEP 1: Gather 1 pound each of butter, sugar, eggs, and flour. Optional: Tb vanilla, tsp salt.
STEP 2: Heat oven to 350°F (175°C).
STEP 3: Beat the butter until it is smooth.
STEP 4: Add the sugar and beat until light and fluffy.
STEP 5: In a separate bowl, beat eggs (Optional: add a tablespoon of vanilla and a teaspoon of salt)
STEP 6: Slowly add eggs, a little at a time, to the butter-sugar mixture. Beat gently with each addition.
STEP 7: Add flour, about ¼ cup at a time, stirring gently until all has been incorporated.
STEP 8: Pour batter into pan and smooth the surface with a spatula.
STEP 9: Bake for about 1 hour 15 minutes. The cake is done when a wooden skewer comes out clean.
STEP 10: Cool for 20 minutes before serving.
Bon Appetit![41]

[41] That's a shoutout to my fellow Pasadena girl, fellow Poly student, Julia Child.

If you know anything about baking, you know that each step matters. It simply wouldn't do to scramble their order. The cake won't bake properly, and you'll be sad.

It's just the same when you write paragraphs. If you're trying to convince someone about something, or explain how something works, you'll want to think carefully about the order in which you give them the information. This is where I often do the most editing (see step 7). Consider how your paragraphs should all be leading, inexorably, inevitably, towards your final conclusion. Just like how the recipe MUST lead to a cake.

5) Link paragraphs together with transitions

It helps the reader understand the role of each paragraph if you remind them with a word or phrase. This can be as short as a single word that starts the topic sentence (e.g. *additionally, furthermore, conversely*). These transition words help with the continuity of your writing, so it doesn't feel like you are rapidly jerking your readers from one unrelated idea to another. Sometimes, you'll find that your transitions are more complicated. In that case, they can stand alone as a sentence or two. For instance:

Now that we have addressed the issues of paragraph construction, we may move on to more general concerns of composition.

6) Be concise.

Feel free to write long, rambling sentences, as long as you're prepared to edit out all the unnecessary words later. To quote that elegant little book *The Elements of Style* by Strunk and White, **OMIT NEEDLESS**

WORDS. I like to write my papers in 3 passes: pre-write, rough draft, final draft. I don't worry so much about being concise in my rough draft, but I am ruthless about cutting unneeded words or phrases in the final draft.

7) Improve your writing by editing.

One of the most wonderful things about *not* writing on my old typewriter is how much easier it is now to edit. After I've written my first draft, I set it aside. Ideally, I let a whole day go by. Then I reread it with fresh eyes. Now it's much easier to catch repeated words or phrases (look for reasonable synonyms in a thesaurus). It's also easier to find places where you can change the order of sentences (see step 4), so your ideas progress logically. You may find you accidentally left out a whole point. You can fill in the gap now.

8) Improve your writing by reading.

I hope you like to read, because you need to read a LOT if you want to be a good writer. Immerse yourself in the works of people who love the written word.[42] This is going to be different from your regular pleasure reading. Read with one eye on *how they do it*. How are they constructing their sentences? How are they convincing you? How are they making you laugh? How are they not losing you when they describe something complicated?

---

[42] Really, read whatever you like, but it does help if you step out of your comfort zone. You can't go wrong with the collected essays of E.B. White, George Orwell, and Dorothy Parker, for starters.

9) Improve your writing by more writing.

It's a pervasive myth that good writers can just wait for inspiration to strike, then sit down at their computer and dash off a perfect story. Ernest Hemingway famously said, "The only kind of writing is rewriting." Good writing is a lot of work, and the best authors will tell you they write every day. As with so many things, it comes down to practice.

Once you get comfortable with these rules of thumb, you'll be able to apply this basic framework to almost any kind of writing assignment. Learn how to do these basic steps, and practice until you do it well—and then never stop practicing. I know you have good ideas. Write a little every day, and soon you'll be able to share them with the world.

CHAPTER FOURTEEN

You Should Go to Summer School

When I was a kid, I went to summer school every year. By choice! Well, it was that or work all day, every day in my mum's shop. At my school's summer program, I got to be in an air-conditioned classroom with other kids for a couple of hours every day, doing "enrichment activities." I don't remember learning anything new—it was all review, to prevent the dreaded "summer slide."[43] Then we'd spend the rest of the day messing around in the school pool, playing Marco Polo and retrieving pennies from the bottom of the deep end. On Tuesdays we'd go to the beach, where we'd alternately burn on the sand and freeze in the Pacific Ocean. On Thursdays we went to the ice skating rink, where I'd twist my ankle and burn my tongue on the vending machine hot chocolate. We took field trips to all the museums and amusement parks in L.A. (Disneyland, Knott's Berry Farm, Universal Studios, Raging Waters, MarineLand, the LA Zoo). Somehow, this was not expensive—kids' tickets were cheap! Ehhh, it was the 80s. Life was good for a kid.

When I look back on it, I realize now that my "summer school" was actually a day camp, but the owners of my school were pretty business savvy and they knew how to sell it to the parents. By calling

---

[43] "Summer slide" is a phenomenon where kids lose some of what they learned during the school year, especially in math and reading skills. If they don't go to summer school, they have to do some review to catch up when school starts again in the fall.

it "summer school," the parents thought it was educational. My parents never would have sent me to *camp*. That was something for the idle wealthy.[44]

I gave up going to summer school the year I turned 16, because I got a full-time job in a lab doing biology research. That was plenty enriching, in more ways than one.[45] I worked every summer after that, because I knew I needed the money for my college tuition. Getting lab experience was also key for my career aspirations. But if you don't have the option to work in your field and save money during your summer break, I think you should go to summer school.[46]

Here's why:

1) **You have to.** Maybe you're *required* to go to summer school, because you failed a class. I know this can feel like the end of the world, but really—it's going to be okay. You'll be amazed how much easier a class feels the second time around, when you already have a feel for where the class is going and what is expected of you. I bet if you refer back to your papers from your first class, they'll make a lot more sense now.

2) **Small class size.** Do you struggle in those giant lecture classes with hundreds of students? Most lower-level college classes (Biology 101, Physics 101, etc.) are run this way. Sadly, they're not the ideal way to learn for most people.[47] You don't always

---

[44] Like Hayley Mills and Hayley Mills in *The Parent Trap*.

[45] Did you get it? *Enriching?* Hehehe! I crack myself up.

[46] And when I say "summer school," I mean *real* summer school, where you take academic classes.

[47] Makes you wonder why colleges all do this, right? Who are the classes for, if not the students?

get to ask questions when you need to. In fact, your instructor may not even know your name. Summer school classes are usually smaller, and you'll be able to get more individualized attention.

3) **Better access to instructors.** As a bonus, by being in a small class, you have a better chance to develop a good working relationship with the instructor. There will be more opportunities for your professor to see just how serious of a student you are. This could lead to an internship, or even someone you trust to write you a letter of recommendation in the future.

4) **Make your life easier during the school year.** There are some classes that are just notoriously difficult (Organic Chemistry, Quantum Mechanics, Anatomy and Physiology—you know what they are for your major). If you're smart about your planning, you can use your summer to focus all your attention on one very time-consuming class. That way, during the school year, you can take a lighter load and have an easier time handling all the rest of your classes.[48]

5) **Save money**. I thought college cost a lot when I went in the 90s. It's *obscenely* expensive now. If there's any way you can avoid paying for some of it, I'd jump on that. So here's the

---

[48] I wish someone had suggested this to me back when I was in college. Honestly, those four years were a blur of sleepless nights and constant struggle. If only I could have taken one fewer class each term, I think it would have made a huge difference. That is, if Caltech would have actually accepted summer classes for credit. I doubt it, since they didn't give any AP credit. Caltech is a very strange, impossible, wonderful place. Don't go there. I'm kidding. But really. It's not for everyone.

plan, if your college accepts it: Graduate in three years instead of four. Take as many AP classes as you can while you're in high school (you'll get 5s on your APs, obviously), to place out of lower-level college classes. Then double down and take some of your college classes at a community college during the summers. It's going to cost you something, but not nearly as much as a year at a four-year institution. This takes some careful planning, but if you could wind up only having to pay for three years of college rather than four, that's a HUGE savings. Like down-payment-on-a-house savings.

6) **Get ahead.** You're really looking forward to taking Clinical Psychology from the world-famous professor at your college, but you have to take stats and freshman composition first. If you know your major requires a whole bunch of prerequisites that aren't that great, why not knock them out during the summer? This goes right along with saving money—you can also save *time* by taking summer classes. If you know for sure what your major is, you could finish your degree faster by getting your prerequisites out of the way. It's also a way to make room in your schedule for more of the good stuff your college has to offer.

I want to end with a serious caveat—don't assume that your summer school class will be a breeze. It won't be anything like *my* summer school experience. Don't sign up hoping for day camp. Summer school is real school, and you should expect to spend *at least* as much time on this class as you would if you took it during the school year. It may be even faster-paced, since summer school classes are often squeezed into fewer weeks. As a result, some summer school classes have extra-long lectures. Can you handle that? It's a different kind of challenge to stay focused on one class for multiple hours at a time. Make sure to take breaks—think Pomodoro, break, Pomodoro, break, Pomodoro, break....

If you want to succeed in your summer school classes, you should apply all the Great Student lessons you've learned from this book. Get a planner. Use it. Take good notes in class, and review them every day. Read your textbook, and take good reading notes. Keep up with your homework. Break your studying into chunks using the Pomodoro technique. Don't cram for your tests—put them in your planner and count backwards a few days, so you know when you need to start studying. Use the Feynman Technique to test your understanding. *You know all this.*

CHAPTER FIFTEEN

How to Take Online Classes

(BONUS PandemicTime Chapter)

I'm writing to you from the very strange year of 2020. We've been quarantined at home since February. I hopped on that train early, at the first whispers that there was a "brand-new killer virus" in the news.[49] That means we've been doing a lot of our work at Socratica virtually, as best as we can. In my normal life, I spend my time tooling around Los Angeles, having filmmaking adventures, writing in coffee shops, going to the beach, haunting libraries and bookstores, going to the movies, visiting friends, and tracking down taco trucks. Instead, I've been sitting in one place most of the year, looking at my own reflection in my computer screen.

I can also see, out my front window, a group of kids that are having the weirdest school year ever. Their PE class consists of riding their little bikes up and down my driveway. Hallowe'en was cancelled—the most important day of the Kid Year. Remember how significant each school year was when you were growing up? They've missed everything. I *can't imagine* what it's like for these kids.

It's got to be weird for college students, too. Are you in college? I kind of assume you are, but I don't know, maybe you're in high school. I

---

[49] As a molecular biologist who specialized in immunology, I have a very healthy fear of deadly pathogens.

would have *jumped* on a book like this when I was fourteen.[50] In any case, if you're in school, you've probably had to deal with taking online classes this year whether you wanted to or not.

I'm going to go out on a limb here and make a prediction. I'm betting that your online classes were really, *really* hard to adjust to. Where was the nice give and take with your instructor? Remember how they would see when everyone was confused, so they'd stop and clarify something? Now, with webcams, no one knows where to look, and we can't easily pick up on facial expressions. Where's the casual banter with your classmates? Remember passing notes? So fun! Maybe that's not so important in college, but still. Now you can't! Online classes have just been a pale imitation of the real thing.

We should remember that online classes never were very successful. Did you know that before the pandemic, online courses had a completion rate of only three percent? THREE PERCENT!! If big online education companies[51] with whole research departments and millions of dollars of investment backing them couldn't figure out how to make online classes successful, it was folly to expect teachers with no training and no experience to throw together something that would work.

I don't want to discount those big online educational companies completely. They represent a LOT of test cases. Let's consider that for a handful of students in each of those online classes, they *were* able to

---

[50] If I could send myself a message when I was starting high school, what would I say? Hey, little Kim from the past. Don't waste any more time trying to be friends with mean kids. And don't take no for an answer when you ask to be moved up to the advanced math class. Also—life is going to get *so* much better.

[51] I figure I shouldn't name names, but you know who they are.

make it work. What sets apart that successful three percent of students?

1) **They treat it like a job.** In other words, your online class is a professional responsibility. You need to show up for work, ready to work. Part of the challenge is that our homes were never meant for school or business. We don't always have an adequate computer setup: big screen monitor, high definition webcam, desk big enough for your computer (monitor, keyboard, mouse) AND a textbook AND a notebook to write in, comfortable ergonomic chair, etc. Look back at the first chapter about setting up your study environment to get some ideas about how to make this work. Also think about sending yourself a signal that you are ready for work by dressing for the job—even if that just means putting on your college sweatshirt.

2) **They log in every day.** Remember what we learned about **Spaced Repetition** and the **Forgetting Curve**? You still have to deal with your forgetful brain when you take an online class. The sooner you come back to the material, the better chance you have of retaining it. Maybe you don't have a choice, and you have to show up for class every day. In that case, *good*, this is a non-issue. But if your class is set up to be asynchronous, meaning you can watch lectures and do activities anytime you choose, it's important that you don't let much time pass between lessons. Don't save them up and try to cram all your work into one day a week. Rather, pick a consistent time every day for attending your class. Write it in your planner so you don't schedule something else at the same time.

3) **They participate**. This may mean different things, depending on how your class is set up. If the class is live, think about how often you offer input via the chat window, or respond verbally to your instructor's questions. The key concept here is **engagement.** If you never participate, your learning is passive and probably less effective. I'm not suggesting that you need to force yourself to speak up even if you don't have something to say. Rather, take advantage of the opportunities you *do* have to be a part of the class dynamic. If there are scheduled office hours, use them (but remember to prepare appropriately using the **Corson Technique**). Some courses have a discussion board, where you'll talk about the class topics outside of the lecture. You may find this an easier way to contribute. In any case, I'm *sure* you have some interesting ideas. Share them with the class!

4) **They're persistent.** Here's the thing. The people who succeed at online classes aren't necessarily the smartest or what we would normally think of as the *best* students. But these are people who are willing to struggle publicly. They don't give up at the first sign of technical difficulties. They don't give up because they aren't getting as much personal attention as they would like. They don't give up because their online class doesn't measure up to an unrealistic expectation. To succeed, you're going to have to find this persistent, flexible, tolerant person inside. *You can do this.*

Be safe and well.
KHH

AFTERWORD

ell, my friends, we've reached the end of our time together. Don't be sad! Anytime you miss me, you can open up this book again and I'll be right here with you, giving you some excellent advice. You can also see my face on YouTube if you're interested in some truly fabulous biology and chemistry videos.[52]

Actually, since I still have you here, I'd like to pass on a few more bits of advice that didn't fit neatly into one of the chapters of this book. These aren't study tips *per se*, but they're life lessons that indirectly helped me grow into a Great Student, and they might help you, too.

1) **Get a job.** I grew up working in my mum's little shop, so I tell people (quite truthfully) that I've been working since I was five years old. My first job was putting together boxes. The next year, I was allowed to sweep the sidewalk in front of the store with a junior-sized broom. As soon as I got good enough at printing numbers (around age 8), I started writing the prices on price tags. When my math skills got to be pretty reliable, I ran the register (age 10) . When I was finally tall enough, I started cleaning out dressing rooms and putting merchandise back up on shelves (age 11). I learned to type and got a typewriter for my 12th birthday, and so the task of writing to customers about their bills fell to me. This is how I spent my

[52] Don't forget to take notes.

childhood, after school and on the weekends. The job grew with me, and I grew with the job.

There's nothing that fuels your self-confidence like doing a proper job well. I truly believe that for the good of society, everyone needs to work retail for at least a year. Working for minimum wage gives you a healthy sense of respect for how hard *everyone* works at their job. You'll see just how many hours of work it takes to bring home a few dollars, making you less likely to waste your paycheck on silly things. It also lets you experience the real financial benefit that can come from education.[53]

2) **Learn to drive.** The day I turned 16, I got my driver's license. A few months later, I bought a car (I had been saving furiously for this day). Now I was able to drive across L.A. to my first job in a lab, which started my career as a research biologist, and allowed me to start seriously saving for my future. Being mobile and independent allows you to take advantage of these kinds of opportunities in your life. I have no doubt that my lab experience made a big difference when it came time for college applications.

3) **Save money.** You might think as a poor kid making real money for the first time in her life, I'd blow it all on trendy clothes and root beer floats. Nope, I spent just what I had to on gas to get to my job. The rest I socked away in an investment account. I knew that in a couple of years, I'd be paying for college. Money opens doors and gives you choices.

---

[53] A college degree is not a guarantee of financial success anymore, I know. But it's still usually a minimum requirement for a lot of professional careers.

4) **Invest in your education.** I am extremely frugal, probably to a fault. But one thing I never deny myself is spending the money I've earned on books and classes and a computer. Buy yourself the tools you need. It's investing in yourself, and investing in your future.

RESOURCES

I've created a page of resources (recommended books, videos, articles, irresistible office supplies) on our website, socratica.com. Go to socratica.com/books/great-student.

You may go directly to the page by using this QR code:

ACKNOWLEDGEMENTS

"The truth is, when all is said and done, one does not teach a subject, one teaches a student how to learn it."

Jacques Barzun

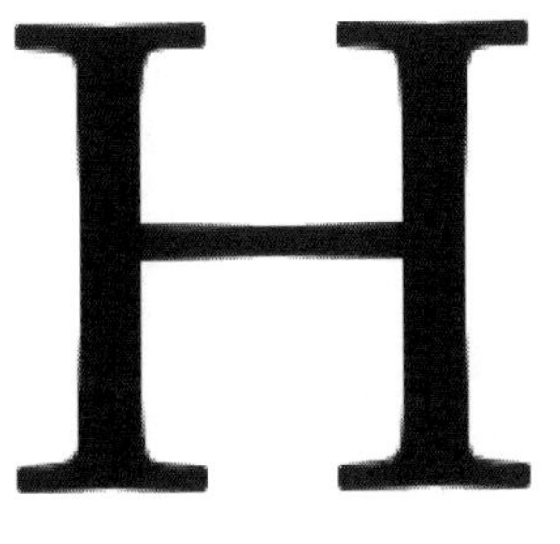ow can I *begin* to thank my teachers. I thought I could write a book, and put them in it. I found by the time I finished, there were not enough pages to mention them all. There were so many of them that sent me off into the world, loading my raft with small gifts. I remember a thousand kindnesses.

Doris Street was my grammar school drama and art teacher. She looked *exactly* like Eleanor Parker as Baroness Von Schraeder from *The Sound of Music.* She was so elegant—like something from another era, with smooth blonde hair coiled on top of her head, silk blouses, pencil skirts, and high heels made for flamenco dancing. She could have been a movie star. But most miraculous of all, she was kind. She was so charming and darkly funny, and never made me feel awkward despite my being a grubby bespectacled tween. Middle school is a terrible time for everyone, but in her classroom I felt cherished. On the day of one of our musical performances, my parents never showed up, and I was left all alone after everyone else went home. She took me out to dinner with her husband. Never made a fuss, never made me feel bad, she just did it. I'm sure I said thank you at the time, but I regret that I never let her know she was a true star in my life.

Kevin Pariseau was my first drama and voice teacher in high school. When I was lost in this terrifying new prep school full of unspoken social rules, he gave me safe harbour. He gave me a part in a play, laughed at all of my jokes, and taught me the importance of a good vocal warm up. In a world full of people who would put me in a small box, he made it okay for me to be both a Humanist and a Scientist. There was one day when he saw me reading my math book. "This, this right here, is going to answer all of your questions in life," he said. Did he know that one day I would marry a tall, dark, handsome mathematician? *Ma may me mo moo.*

Faith Conger was my yoga teacher for five years when I was in grad school. She was the one person at Princeton who listened and understood why I was leaving science research to become a teacher. Her gentle guidance brought me great peace during that tumultuous time. More than *asanas* and *pranayama,* she taught me by how she moved gracefully through life. One day she came to class with her foot bandaged. She told us she was rushing to class and tripped, twisting her ankle. Rather than being angry at God and the Universe, she explained how it was a teachable moment. She learned she needed to slow down, both literally and metaphorically. We had no idea of her age—because she was quite simply ageless—but when Fred Rogers died, she shared how they had a long friendship that started back in her freshman year of college. She was a quiet little ghost, she said, so sad and withdrawn about her mother passing, and he very kindly took her as his special guest to his senior recital, and made her feel that there were still good things in the world. It made perfect sense that my beautiful angelic teacher was friends with Mr. Rogers.

I picture a crew of guardian angel teachers who accompany me through life, something like the glowing figure of Obi Wan who looked after Luke Skywalker. Along with my own teachers, there are Mr. Rogers (friend of a friend status), Carl Sagan, Richard Feynman, E.B. White, Julia Child, Joseph Campbell, Ray Bradbury.

When I became a teacher, it opened my eyes to what kind of student I had been. I saw myself and my own struggles reflected back at me—not much changes about classroom life, even across the decades. Teaching allowed me to step outside myself and appreciate my own evolution as a student. I could see with a new clarity what was working, and where so much mental energy was wasted. I couldn't go back and offer help to myself in the past, but I could use my new insights to help the students in front of me in my own classroom. My teaching colleagues helped me gain this understanding, and I will be forever grateful for their companionship and the sadder-but-wiser laughter we shared. How beautiful it was to graduate into their ranks.

ABOUT THE AUTHOR

Kimberly Hatch Harrison was born and raised in Pasadena, California—a place known for flowers in winter, elaborate parades, closet millionaires, and world-class educational institutions. Stubborn and ingenious, she refused to be broken by those same educational institutions that would tame her. A child prodigy, she taught herself to read somewhere around the age of 2½. She credits her mother for instilling her lifelong love of reading, which made everything else possible.

Kimberly attended (the now defunct) Pasadena Towne & Country School, the exclusive prep school Pasadena Polytechnic (formerly Throop Institute), and the uber-exclusive Caltech (also formerly Throop Institute). She earned bachelor's degrees in Biology and English Literature from Caltech. She continued her studies in Molecular Biology at Princeton, leaving grad school with a masters degree and ABD (all but dissertation) as a PhD candidate. After spending 16+ years doing science research, she came full-circle back to Pasadena to teach biology and chemistry at Polytechnic School, finally leaving in a blaze of glory to co-found Socratica with her tall, dark, and handsome husband.

Kimberly lives in Los Angeles.

Follow Kimberly at
www.socratica.com
youtube.com/socratica
twitter.com/SocraticaKim

Made in the USA
Middletown, DE
10 September 2024